STEWART LEE

Stewart <u>Lee!</u>
The *If You Prefer a Milder Comedian, Please Ask for One* EP

faber and faber

First published in 2012
by Faber and Faber Ltd
Bloomsbury House
74–77 Great Russell Street
London WC1B 3DA

Typeset by Ian Bahrami
Printed and bound by CPI Group (UK) Ltd, Croydon, CR0 4YY

A CIP record for this book
is available from the British Library

ISBN 978–0–571–27984–5

2 4 6 8 10 9 7 5 3 1

To my mother, Maureen Lee

Contents

Introduction

The first series of *Stewart Lee's Comedy Vehicle*, a mixture of as-live stand-up and filmed sketches, had a troubled birth. Initially, it had been commissioned in full by the BBC in 2005, and then cancelled before work had begun on it in 2006, before being given a pilot in 2007, and finally a six-part series in 2008. The events surrounding this, and the three stand-up shows that led up to it, are detailed in my first book about stand-up, *How I Escaped My Certain Fate*. View that book as a 12″ vinyl album, such as The Specials' 1979 debut, and this as a complementary EP, such as *The Special AKA Live!*, with live tracks and otherwise unavailable tunes, and issued after the album's release to exploit consumer interest in the first product while a more substantial follow-up is prepared. There will be more thoughts on television, stand-up and the toxic mix of the two in my next book, *TV Comedian* (available summer 2012 from all good bookshops).

Stewart Lee's Comedy Vehicle was shot between December 2008 and January 2009, and broadcast in April of that year, to almost universal approval from the broadsheets and intermittent praise from the tabloids. Viewing figures climbed to near the one and a quarter million mark, a respectably high figure these days. Excerpts of the programme were shown at broadcasting-industry conferences and think tanks as an example of what contemporary TV comedy could be doing.

While the series was being broadcast, I kept my head down, trying to avoid both praise and blame. I quit the country and went to a Center Parcs in Normandy, where my family and I ate boiled eggs for breakfast every day by an artificial lake full of grey dishwater. Meanwhile, the series' producer and director, Richard Webb and Tim Kirkby respectively, basked in the unexpected acclaim, like pigs in shit. The approval of our peers rained down upon us in an endless golden shower. A second series seemed certain. Then the executives that had commissioned the show left BBC2 for Sky and BBC1, and the unprecedentedly acclaimed *Stewart Lee's Comedy Vehicle* was immediately mothballed by the incoming regime. My new agent Debi Allen, who had re-established relations between me and the BBC, saw her understandable delight turning to despair and was professionally distraught. I, however, took an almost perverse pleasure in the fact that my adventure in broadcasting seemed once again to be turning predictably sour.

The money from the TV series meant that my wife Bridget and I could get a mortgage and stay in London, as everyone should, with a room for the boy, a room for me to work in and rack with bookshelves, and another to fill up with stuff that you never get round to using – the kind of quasi-mythical architectural space that would serve as the perfect subject for a Michael McIntyre-style routine, should I ever suffer a personality disorder and write one.* We had a sofa to sit on and a table to eat off now, and

---

* Apparently, the family of the TV producer Robert Popper call their own equivalent of this space 'the pig's room'.

wondered how we had managed for so long without them. We could not go back to the old days, with our cushions and our trough. And with my vain table and my conceited shelves, I was already living beyond my wildest dreams, though my wildest dreams had only ever extended as far as the hope, as Harry Hill once described his own highest ambition, that I would not die alone in rented accommodation. Newly philosophical and content, my short-term objectives fulfilled, I rationalised easily the end of the sudden Indian summer of my small-screen success. In my mind, it was I that had proudly abandoned television once more, rather than it abandoning me, and whereas in the nineties I would have sat in pubs howling 'WHY??!!' and choking back potato crisps through a salty haze of bitter tears, I instead shrugged off BBC2's indecisiveness and set my shoulder to the wheel of developing a new live show.

What to do onstage next presented five distinct problems. Firstly, given that upwards of a million people had enjoyed the television series, would I now be playing to audiences principally composed of punters that knew what to expect from me; and if so, would I now be trusted to go further than usual with form and content, and if so, how far? Or would my new status as 'television comedian' mean that casual consumers expecting *Comedy Roadshow*-type recognition fun would continue to be snagged accidentally, and thus create extra pockets of resistance in every room?

Secondly, since my return in 2004 I had enjoyed a convenient outsider/failure status: the acclaimed live show I contributed to, *Jerry Springer: The Opera*, had ended in financial ruin and a right-wing Christian witch hunt, and my proposed TV series had been abandoned thanks to the fluctuating whims of the BBC. But such status-lowering failures allowed me to snipe at people from without the citadel of success, like a comedian should. Now, however, I was back on television. To the casual observer I was suddenly a powerful figure of sorts, to all intents and purposes a denizen of the same sequinned world as many of the glitzy celebrities I sneer at for money. My wife had alerted me to the danger of this, and the hundreds of viewers who posted online that they thought the TV me was smug* confirmed that, to quote the long-lost nineties stand-up Jason Freeman, context is not a myth. Could I engineer a deliberate lowering of status in a new live show that would enable me to persevere with the social and celebrity satire elements of what I did without looking like a conceited, arrogant bully?

The third problem is a by-product of both the above. An audience member who only knows stand-up from television probably has little real experience of what a stand-up show is. As a result, the TV comedian's gig is often, and through no fault of the performer, less like a comedy show and more like a prolonged personal appearance. I saw the immediate post-heroin Russell Brand, with his golden highlighted hair, do some impressive sets in rooms above North London pubs in the mid-noughties. But from what I can glean by watching short out-of-context extracts from his DVDs on television late at night when I am drunk, it seems that today his stand-up shows are more like celebrity walkabouts – pee-generating incidents and bra-harvesting opportunities with

* 'Smug elitist liberalism. Who is this cunt?' Tokyofist, on YouTube. 'His whole tone is one of complete, smug condescension,' *Birmingham Sunday Mercury*. 'His smug attitude and the fact that he comes across like a grade A bellend makes him unwatchable for me,' Joycey33, readytogo.net. 'I always thought Stuart Lee was a smug, unfunny, my view's right and if you disagree you're wrong, right on lefty, cunt,' MadDog, westhamonline.com. Etc., etc.

comedy thrown in. Who knows what kind of performer Brand may have developed into had success and acclaim not robbed him of the opportunity to evolve unmolested? A less wealthy and even better one, perhaps.

For my own sake, and for the audience's, I did not want things to be too easy. What could I do to make a new stand-up show difficult and alienating enough to guarantee that any TV viewers coming along for the first time were sufficiently bamboozled and bewildered to respond to the material and performance on their own merits? How could I shake them off, bore them, annoy them, but still pull them back in for the final reel? How could I make them feel part of a living performance process, rather than simply being onlookers at a minor celebrity spectacle?

Fourthly, in the year I'd been working on the TV show live comedy had become bigger business still. Even journalists had noticed this and were beginning to wish they hadn't squandered the phrase 'Comedy Is the New Rock and Roll' back in the early nineties, when it was in fact just the new spacedust. For me, lots of sell-outs on the last tour meant that this time around I was, on occasion, to be booked into rooms that held more than a thousand paying people; not a huge figure in the modern stand-up scheme of things, but a vast one by my standards. How could I twist what I did, based as it often was on a kind of intimidating and embarrassing intimacy – a relative *lack* of success – to fit those rooms?

And fifthly, it was already springtime. The deadlines for tour dates and the Edinburgh Fringe were approaching, and I'd just turned two hours of brand-new material, plus an hour or so of old unused scrapings and off-cuts, into a TV series. What was I going to talk about now? Where was this show going to come from?

I was mulling this over as I wheeled my sleeping son's pram from central London up to Camden and lunch with my live promoter, when an incident in an Oxford Street coffee shop seemed to suggest a starting point for a new show. Even though I know it's wrong, I am a regular and indiscriminate consumer of high-street coffee-chain coffee. I went into the Oxford Street Caffè Nero, pushing my pram and waving my loyalty card. But the fact that three of the nine stamps were red and the rest were blue was queried by the *barista*, who denied me my free coffee on the grounds that the three non-standard red stamps may have been faked.

The purpose of the lunch with my live promoter was to decide a title for my forthcoming tour. I left the Caffè Nero in a huff, un-caffeinated, but as I traipsed north towards Camden I began to imagine how a TV observational comedian would deal with this mishap. He would speculate as to how and why the *barista* assumed he had faked the stamps, I thought, as I passed the now-closed Fitzrovian hang-out The Black Horse on Rathbone Place. He would wonder what would be the point of only faking three of them instead of all nine, I decided, as I headed up Charlotte Street and past various production companies, where Channel 4 filler is fermented in giant vats. As I crossed the street grid in a north-westerly direction to skim the eastern edge of Regent's Park, via Albany Road, where Edward Lear once lived, sketching parrots from the zoo, I worked through ever more exaggerated responses to the incident in my head. Against my instinct, I began, as I passed The Dublin Castle and the pet shop on Parkway, to find the whole idea genuinely funny.

But it wasn't me. At its simplest it was, like the spare-room idea, a Michael McIntyre bit, ringing bells of recognition in the brains of millions of ordinary people, and in the laughing mouths, too, of celebrities like Gok Wan or Esther Rantzen, down the front at the Hammersmith Apollo, captured by a camera lens. At best it was a Rhod Gilbert routine, whose early surreal style still survives in ghost form in the exaggerated reactions he has to motorway service station mince pies and quilts. Still, though I found the idea funny, I couldn't see myself performing material like this.

I was forty-two years old. I didn't want to do observational comedy. I didn't want to do shock for shock's sake, as was increasingly the fashion, having already reached my personal elastic limit of comedy horror when I discussed vomiting into the gaping anus of Christ for half an hour (in my popular 2005 live show, *'90s Comedian*). I didn't want to do surreal whimsy, as I no longer had the hair or the legs for it; talking about voles and moonbeams, I would look like someone's dad pogoing at a wedding. But I did want to do stand-up, as opposed to theatre. The dignified confessional monologues of the doughty Daniel Kitson, or even the beatific Ben Moor, wonderful as they were, were not for me. I was a turn, and the previous show, *41st Best Stand-Up Ever*, had been about me embracing that, happily. But what kind of turn was I if I was too self-conscious to allow myself to do a funny routine about a coffee-shop loyalty card, something even people in Carlisle might like?

And there, I realised, was the framing device for the new show. What kind of comedian are you? What does being a comedian mean? What can we talk about? As I wheeled the pram past The Good Mixer – where, throughout the Britpop years, the toilet cubicles were always occupied – I got out the Caffè Nero loyalty card and looked at the small print. Squirrelled away between the blue and white blocks of the company's distinctive corporate livery was the phrase: 'If you prefer a milder coffee please ask for one.' By the time I met my promoter outside the Japanese restaurant, I had a poster design etched inside my eyelids, and a title that would seem to say something about the axiomatic modern dilemma facing the contemporary commercial comedian. Family-friendly funster or bile-spewing hate merchant? *If You Prefer a Milder Comedian, Please Ask for One.*

So we had a title. All I needed now was some material. I would get to work straight away. But then my son woke up. So we went to the zoo instead, my promoter breathless with excitement, unused to the act of walking and thrilled by the challenge his scarcely relevant feet presented him.

My usual system for working up new shows was to start doing twenty-minute sets at little North London clubs from about May onwards. I could see what stuck, discover how the material fitted together and establish through-lines for the full show. In addition to which, now that I had a child and less time to stare into dead space wondering about nothing, a lot of my stand-up writing was getting done onstage rather than at a desk. To anyone who queried it, I passed off this more improvisational, conversational style as a positive choice rather than a virtue drawn from necessity. However, in the pre-Edinburgh period of 2009, it became much harder to do all the normal London comedy-scene gigs that I'd done five nights a week in the nineties and had played easily as recently as a year or two before.

There is an understood convention in listings for circuit gigs that if one of the people on the bill is described as 'An Act Who Cannot Be Named', it's probably someone off the telly doing new stuff. I always found this arrangement questionable, as often the person who could not be named would be someone whose name I didn't even know, and whose perception of themselves as someone who could not be named was revealed perhaps as premature, as they stood before a quietly baffled audience, all squinting as they tried to remember where they might remember the unnameable name from. Insisting on being anonymous seemed self-aggrandising, so I was just listed under my own name as normal, because I am modest and saintly. But the TV series, and even the raised level of interest in me prior to it, had changed things at grass roots level. Expectations were significantly higher.*

More irritatingly, there was now Twitter, and portable internet technology, to monitor one's every move. When I was running in material for the television series, I would come out of a gig in some Islington pub, and there were already people in the street outside using their iPhones to upload instantly their opinions on barely baked new bits onto comedy message boards and social networks. By the time I got home, something tentative I had only dreamed up that afternoon was already being eviscerated online. Generating a new show under this kind of scrutiny proved to be a struggle.

Nonetheless, I was fortunate that during the run-up to a month of tryouts of *If You Prefer . . .* at The Stand in Edinburgh, various events suggested material that

---

* Another laughable example of the assumption of anonymity is seen on a caption beneath a photo of a corpse-paint-faced Nordic rock musician in the book *Lords of Chaos: The Bloody Rise of the Satanic Metal Underground* by Michael Moynihan and Didrik Søderlind (Feral House). It reads: "'It' of Abruptum – Too evil to have a human name.' The Australian foole Greg Fleet found this text especially amusing as, as well as 'wool', 'human' is one of the words he considers to have a magical comedy energie.

dovetailed with the overarching theme of what kind of comedian one should be. Like a believer who sees random phenomena as signs from above, it appeared to me as if events were organising themselves to suit my chosen themes. It was in this period, for example, that Michael McIntyre and Frankie Boyle were emerging as the twin pillars of post-Alternative Comedy, both providing multi-platform content to presumably different but similarly large mainstream audiences. As comedians, McIntyre and Boyle defined each other in opposition; as market forces, they were strangely similar.

You could take Michael McIntyre home to meet your granny. You couldn't take Frankie Boyle home to meet your granny because he would rape her and then callously wipe the blood off his penis with a dead kitten before heading off to a corporate Christmas do. McIntyre articulated things you hadn't realised you thought. Boyle articulated things you thought but didn't feel you ought to articulate. A troubled and evidently conscience-stricken man, clearly concerned that he is meant for better things than panel-show sound bites, Boyle was nonetheless becoming popular with the sort of teeth-gnashing types who think political correctness has gone mad. A belated fuss over Boyle's *Mock the Week* joke about the Queen's vagina being advanced in years had meant that the BBC's Emily Maitlis had recently been obliged to say the phrase 'I'm so old my pussy is haunted' over and over again in a cross voice on *Newsnight*. For this alone, Boyle may be forgiven most of his assumed sins.

But, conversely, Boyle was also to become a high-profile columnist for the *Sun*, which had somehow, on this occasion, chosen to accommodate him as the acceptable face of the unacceptable, rather than to demonise him, which would be their usual approach. Was this what a comedian was supposed to be, a kind of tabloid-endorsed merchant of offensive jokes of 140 characters or less? Or was McIntyre the ideal archetype, a bundle of fun who would never posit the idea of a haunted royal reproductive organ, or of any reproductive organ at all, accursed or not, unless he were to happen unexpectedly across it, severed and oozing gore, in his man drawer? *If You Prefer . . .* ought at least to acknowledge these two creepingly definitive archetypes. And if I played to audiences of casual consumers, it was the McIntyre/Boyle models that they would have already accepted as the 'correct' modes of doing stand-up. Perhaps if I was seen to assimilate and then reject them, these punters would come with me as I moved sideways from them. (Note I said 'sideways from' and not 'beyond'. We're all part of the comedy brotherhood. There are no winners in stand-up. We are all losers.)

The McIntyre part of the debate was covered by the coffee-shop card idea. Helpfully for me, in early July – in other words, at the last minute – Boyle gave the following quote in an interview: 'You know what it is – after forty, very few comedians are very good. Very few anybodies are good at anything. The focus really goes.' I feel most artists improve with age, but then I would, as I am an ageing artist, and so are all the people I've invested in emotionally for the last thirty years. I can sympathise with Boyle's point of view, though, and I doubt it was meant entirely seriously. The onstage Stewart Lee, however, afraid of his burgeoning irrelevance, could seize upon this comment and be desperate to prove the outrageous Frankie Boyle wrong. It offered the perfect opportunity to address the idea of the comedian as shock-monger, and to provide the show's much-needed 'jeopardy'. I would be a man fighting his obsolescence, taking issue with his perceived irrelevance.

Further opportunities to define myself in opposition to the anti-PC market, and to court a constituency of disgruntled liberals with money to spend, suggested themselves later the same month. The car writer and humorist Jeremy Clarkson had described the prime minister, Gordon Brown, as a cunt during an off-air studio warm-up for *Top Gear*, perhaps in an attempt to show BBC2's new controller, the duly present Janice Hadlow, who really ran things around here. Hadlow subsequently criticised Clarkson for the comment, whilst praising *Top Gear* itself.* Similarly, earlier in the year, while on a *Top Gear* jaunt to Australia, the car-liking trouser man had called Gordon Brown 'a one-eyed Scottish idiot' on live television. Clarkson's right to mock a cunt's blindness was vigorously defended by the usual suspects, and reluctantly accepted by right-thinking folk too, but it seemed to me to be a further outgrowth of the whole 'outrageous' comedy debate. (And for the purposes of argument let's call Clarkson a comedian, even though I accept he also has a lucrative sideline in car books and borderline racist generalisations.)

And finally, throughout the summer of 2009, it was nigh on impossible to escape the pornographically baffled face of the young Welsh comedian Mark Watson, who was now hawking Magners cider in a series of self-consciously quirky TV ads. In Edinburgh in 2004, Watson's *24 Hour Show* had been quietly inspirational to me in its sheer idiotic audacity and the good-natured hysteria it created;

* *Top Gear* is a huge money-spinner for the BBC and therefore is understandably allowed more leeway in these sorts of matters than less financially significant shows.

watching Watson, the king foole, preside over it had been one of the things that made me glad to be part of a stand-up scene where such things were happening. Watson also wore T-shirts with cool things on them, like weird slogans and pictures of dead philosophers, like I used to, so I had him pegged as one of those left-field alternative indie-type guys, like I imagined I was when I was young. Consequently I was surprised to see him doing an advert. In the eighties, if you were a vaguely alternative band or comedian, dallying with advertising would mean, to cite the oft-quoted Bill Hicks line, that you were 'off the artistic roll call for ever'. But the values of today's young alternative artists, for better or worse, are not those of my generation, who may, it is fair to say, have long been up their own backsides anyway, with their values and ideas. Today, getting an advert is just another step on the career ladder, and I appreciate I may have been alone in being saddened by the young Celt's good fortune.*

Was Watson right to do the advert? I bore him no personal malice – I don't really know him, and tend to like all Welsh people enormously anyway – but the onstage, condescending, morally upstanding Stewart Lee would be furious with the Welsh Whore. And the whole Magners thing was too good to resist. It seemed like there could be hours of stuff in this.

* When I saw Mark Watson hanging off some scaffolding in Edinburgh's New Town in August 2010, orchestrating a promotional happening for one of his books and wearing a yellow hard hat, I ran into The Stand to buy a bottle of Magners to spray over him. The comedians Alan Cochrane and Daniel Kitson were outside and I thought they'd come with me and join in, but they just looked at me as if I were an idiot and seemed to pity me for my pranksome idea. Times have changed.

Finally, in terms of form rather than content, the TV show had, as a result of its comparatively tight twenty-nine-minute time slot, pushed me back towards writing shorter bits. I found the process of grinding out a few minutes of punchy opening gags for the top of each episode especially draining, and had ended up renting all Simon Munnery's best lines off him on a timeshare basis just to get the job done. People who didn't like *Comedy Vehicle* had complained about the lack of jokes. I resolved to meet their criticisms head on, by writing as few jokes as possible for the new tour and aiming to go in the opposite direction to the TV show, towards maybe just two or three ideas, explored at maximum length. Ideally, *If You Prefer . . .* would not have a single quotable line or joke, just vast textural blocks defined by their tone rather than their line-for-line content. I would try to take the casual TV viewer into an area of stand-up they would have been unlikely to encounter.

Hanging over all these ideas about content and structure, however, remained one disconcerting shadow: the sheer size of the spaces I would be playing. On the last two tours, for *'90s Comedian* and *41st Best Stand-Up Ever*, I had had the fourth-wall-defying antics of Julian Cope, Johnny Vegas and the Russian clowns Derevo in mind when I experimented with leaving the stage. I was aware that wandering around the auditorium was in danger of becoming a cliché of my work, but nonetheless I held onto it as an option at the back of my mind as the show developed. The punk painter Billy Childish has talked about his live work with his various garage-punk bands in similar terms: 'The difference between us and the others is that we are trying to close the fifteen-yard gap between us and the audience,' he said, 'and they are trying to open it.' Billy eschews the use of the house PA for onstage amps, drawing the audience towards him. Similarly, students of variety will show you clips of Max Miller leaning conspiratorially across the lip of the stage, gesturing back to the space behind him as if the show is something separate from both him and the audience. Perhaps I could trick myself into thinking of the stage itself, in these bigger rooms, as a cage to be escaped from, and go further out than I had before. Just as my response to the criticism that I had no jokes was to try and do none, maybe the correct response to an anxiety that in roving the aisles I was going over old ground was simply to do it even more.

So, in the run-up to *If You Prefer* . . . Frankie Boyle had dismissed ageing comics, Jeremy Clarkson had ignited another debate about taste and comedy and cruelty, and Mark Watson had done a cider advert. All three seemed relevant to the idea of what comedy was and what it was for, and to the idea of what a comedian was supposed to be. Perhaps *If You Prefer* . . . could expand massively the ground covered in the closing few minutes of *41st Best* . . ., when I put a toy giraffe on my head in honour of my little boy and asked the audience to consider the gesture a sincere one. It seemed that today, Alternative Comedians could say anything they liked about anyone and even do adverts with impunity. In 2009, what was the last taboo? Perhaps it was saying something you really meant.

If You Prefer a Milder Comedian,
Please Ask for One

A transcript of the show recorded on 15 March 2010
at the Citizens Theatre, Glasgow

LOUD MUSIC: 'I AM A TREE' BY GUIDED BY VOICES. FLASHING LIGHTS. CLOUDS OF DRY ICE. THE STAGE IS BARE SAVE FOR A MICROPHONE STAND, A STOOL AND, AT THE BACK OF THE STAGE, A GUITAR. MORE DRY ICE BILLOWS FROM THE WINGS.*

* The brief for the pre-show music was simpler than in previous years. I wanted to ape the rock-and-roll mood established by a whole new generation of trim-buttocked, knock-kneed, thirty-something, *Roadshow*-spawned comedians, but make it look absurd. The big landfill indie-rock tunes and dry-ice entrance have become ubiquitous in twenty-first-century UK TV stand-up and the massive stand-up tours that it sustains, though Bill Hicks's arrival onstage in a column of flame in the early nineties, to the sound of strangulated Hendrixisms, probably helped prepare the ground. People no longer even wonder about whether it's appropriate for a comedian to enter like a rock star. It's a default setting, like oompah music for clowns or honking sax solos for forties broads in black stockings. On ITV's *Comedy Rocks* even Jason Manford now emerges from clouds of tastefully distorted power chords and smoke, before talking engagingly about shopping trolleys to the compliant fake indie-rock house band.

To that end, I made a pre-show compilation of tracks by Guided by Voices, who fulfil the demand that rock music should rock, whilst at the same time fracturing even their simplest songs with lo-fi noise and idiot-savant gestures, sounding like olde US power-poppers The Knack if they'd been fronted by the Aspergic visionary

VOICE OFF: Ladies and gentlemen, if you prefer a milder comedian, please ask for one and welcome Stewart Lee.

Thank you very much. Thank you, thank you. Er . . . I'm Stewart Lee. Now, er, later on . . .

[*Stew notices that the dry ice has billowed upwards and is obscuring much of the stage.*]*

Henry Darger. 'I Am a Tree' offers one of the great guitar riffs of all time. It would be quite simply impossible for any mere stand-up comedian to live up to the challenge it throws down. Crank it up as a fanfare and disappointment is ensured.

* While the track was playing, I would be crouched in the wings pumping dry ice onto the stage out of a small portable unit my promoter had found under a desk in his office. I rejected the bigger theatres' offers of using their in-house smoke generators as I wanted, each night, to judge just the right wrong amount of smoke personally, to be able to direct it myself through the unit's funnel to just slightly the wrong areas of the stage, in just slightly the wrong quantities. I wanted to sabotage my own big rock-and-roll opening perfectly. But, of course, smoke, being smoke, remained unpredictable when mixed with air and rarely gathered where I wanted it to, meaning its positioning for the opening, though wrong, was rarely wrong in a way I wanted it to be. Which was ideal. Every night I began the show in a state of panic, improvising around the variables caused by the smoke. Of course, by the time the show this transcript was taken from was recorded, I had improvised around the random smoke so many times that a number of decision-tree options have fallen into place, but it was still a stimulating start.

Having contrived a way of having an exciting rock-and-roll opening, I imagine it will now be very difficult to retreat from it. On the next tour I expect to emerge to a Joan Jett number in a fusillade of flash bombs, without any gloss of irony. It's inevitable. All successful stand-ups, all artists, eventually become the actual thing they began by parodying. That is their tragedy. It is why they all hate themselves and want to die. If you are a young comic reading

What the . . . Oh, that hasn't worked, has it? It's supposed to be, er . . . [*gestures below the knee*] like, like there. Oh dear, y'know, I'm sorry. There's people there going like that. [*waves hand*] What normally happens is . . . Oh, no. What normally happens is, it's down there and I come, I come through, and there's all fast music and lights, and I come through it. It's like, er, one of these, er, young Russell comics that they have now, would have that. They'd come through, and, er . . .*

It's all . . . It's basically, it's gone all up there. But I'm not up there, I'm down here. And er . . .†

I'll go off and I'll just start the . . . I'll just start without the, er . . .

[*Stew exits stage right.*]‡

VOICE OFF: If you prefer a milder comedian, please ask for one and welcome Stewart Lee!

[*Stew enters.*]

---

this and are worried that you have sold out, or may sell out at some point, DO IT! KILL YOURSELF NOW! And tell 'em down below that I sent ya!

* 'These young Russell comics that they have now' is basically how my semi-fictional gran, whom we previously encountered when confused by that political correctness gone mad, would understand stand-up in the UK in 2009.

† Conventional wisdom says we should start with a great gag. Instead, I tried to say as little as possible in as many words as possible. I tried each night to be as unfunny as I could, to appear as if I had no grasp of the situation whatsoever.

‡ Once again, we have the empty stage. Some nights I could spend a minute or so off here, waiting for the room to quieten down again. This whole multiple entrance routine was never written; it just evolved over the course of the tour until it semi-settled.

Thank you very much. Thank you, Glasgow. Thank you. I'm Stewart Lee.

Now, like me, you probably have a favourite high-street coffee retail outlet. [*to audience member in front row*] What's yours? Your favourite high-street coffee retail outlet?

AUDIENCE MEMBER: Costa.

Costa. Why is that?

AUDIENCE MEMBER: [*inaudible*]

It's the first one that came into your head. What? It's the first one that came into your head and . . . And you panicked. [*troubled*] Ohh . . .*

What normally happens is I, I come through . . . and er . . . then, then I say . . . to someone, 'What's your favourite high-street coffee retail outlet?' And they say one, and I say, 'Why is that?' And normally the reason is . . . There's some facts in it and I can . . . And I come off . . . It's not your fault you didn't know that it was . . . But I normally, normally I come off the back of it . . . and I do about ten, fifteen seconds sort of semi-prepared kind of improv off that. And then I work round to what I want to talk about, which is, er, [*produces Caffè Nero loyalty card from top pocket*] Caffè Nero. I want to talk about Caffè Nero.†

---

* Here, the trick was to attack the beginning of the audience-interaction bit as if it were a tried and tested opening that always worked, but I was secure in the knowledge that 90 per cent of the time the chosen audience member would give me nothing to work with; even if they came up with something funny, I could contrive a way of making our dialogue stall. Then I would gather my skirts and begin again.

† Here I give away deliberately what ought to be the surprise conclusion of the opening routine, namely the reveal of the Caffè Nero card, meaning that the laugh it gets on its later arrival will be about

There's a Caffè Nero card there [*shows Caffè Nero card to front row and puts it back in pocket*]. But, um, I like to disguise it, as if it's just come out of a little chat, you know. 'Cause it struck me recently that the whole idea of a, of a stand-up just beginning a set is very contrived, isn't it? You just sort of come out and you suddenly volunteer an opinion about something, apropos of nothing. If you had a friend that did that, you'd think they were really . . . If you had a friend and you went, 'Hello.' And he went, 'Hello. I dislike wool.' You'd go, 'That's why you . . .'*

So I've tried to make it . . . But here in Glasgow the people are very . . . They're not . . . You're not giving, are you? You're not giving. It's just like . . . I don't know. Now the smoke's all gone and I haven't got . . . I'll go off and then I'll . . . I'll just come out and I'll just go into straight talking. I'll just come on and I'll immediately talk about the . . . Forget this. And anyway, he was supposed to film that anyway, and he's right up there. So that won't even . . . won't register anything. [*Stew exits stage right, muttering to himself*] It's a fucking waste of time.

VOICE OFF: Glasgow, if you prefer a milder comedian, please ask for one and welcome Stewart Lee!

[*Stew enters.*]

Hey! Glasgow, Citizens Theatre. What a pleasure to be

———

the inevitability of its telegraphed appearance. Is it possible to be funny, still, when one has ruined all one's jokes?

* I suppose on some level what I am doing here is trying to tell any stray punters, hoovered up in the slipstream of me being on TV, that I am not one of those comics who come out and volunteer such opinions, so they may as well stop waiting for one to come.

here. I'm Stewart Lee and my favourite high-street coffee retail outlet is Caffè Nero.*

Now, there's two reasons, Glasgow, why I like Caffè Nero, which I must admit . . . the cheers for it there, it's never been so warmly received in any other part of the country as it is here, where in Glasgow, typically, there's a very sectarian attitude towards coffee outlets. The Caffè Nero fans over there. The Costa fans over here. Never the twain shall meet.†

Caffè Nero. Now, there's two reasons I like Caffè Nero. First of all, I like Caffè Nero 'cause I often go there in the company of a small two-year-old boy, and they've never once refused to warm his milk. I should point out at this juncture, Glasgow, Citizens Theatre, that the two-year-old boy is my son. I've not been going out socially with a two-year-old boy. Oh no! And if I was, I wouldn't take him to Caffè Nero, would I, madam? That's not the kind of thing they like, coffee and bread and napkins.‡ The sort of thing

---

* This sentence gets a laugh because the audience have constructed a little narrative in their own heads, whereby it's intimated that I was supposed to arrive at the subject of Caffè Nero by a funny route, which is never revealed, and which has now been abandoned anyway. They are laughing at the absence of a joke, the exact nature of which is left up to their own imaginations.

† I love playing Glasgow. There are so many local details to have fun with and it adds an extra frisson to be an English person in the city, apparently behaving with provocative disrespect.

‡ Here I am deliberately moving into a sort of faux-McIntyre mode, trying to sell this everyday material with a kind of jaunty confidence. I really enjoyed doing this and, like the characters in the Raymond Carver story who end up wearing the clothes of the holidaying neighbours whose house they were supposed to be looking after, I had a brief taste of what it might be like to live another man's life.

a little two-year-old boy . . . A tip for you, if you have to entertain one, take them to these places, right, they're normally called things like Pirates' Adventure Castle or Pirates' Adventure Activity Centre, and they're, er, in old warehouses and they're, they're full of all the pirate stuff that little boys like, all the pirate stuff, like rigging you can climb up, all the pirate stuff. And masts you can slide down, all the pirate stuff. And, um, tanks full of blue plastic balls, all the pirate stuff, like they had in the piracy times, on the Spanish main, the tank of blue plastic balls. And little boys love them.*

But conversely, the Pirates' Adventure Castle Activity Centre is a terrible place, Glasgow, to go out socially with a pirate. You'd think they'd love it, wouldn't you? But for a pirate, a visit to the Pirates' Adventure Castle Activity Centre is very much a busman's holiday, as I learned to my shame and regret upon the receipt of this furious letter.

* After having a child in 2007, I determined that I would not be the sort of comic who ended up writing material about children – there are other people far better suited to it – but the more optimistic bent of *41st Best Stand-Up Ever* was clearly a result of fatherhood's cynicism-dissolving side effects. Here I am in character, in a way, as a kind of BBC1/ITV comedian doing dad stuff, the conceit being that I can't quite pitch it correctly and become hamstrung in my quest for mainstream popularity by the inclusion of inappropriately left-field detail. That said, I am spending a lot of time at Pirates' Adventure Castle Activity Centres these days, and worry that the hours we enjoy in them are giving my son an inaccurate impression of pirates as men who eschewed rape, pillage and theft for nautical-themed gymnastic activities, and who always took their shoes off before going on a ship so they didn't kick any of the other pirates in the eye. In a parallel universe, pirates are celebrating their birthdays at Toddlers' Adventure Activity Centres, sitting on crash mats in nappies, screaming.

[*produces folded-up piece of paper from jacket pocket*]*

'Dear Stewart. I thought we could be friends, but it appears not. You took me, a pirate, to a Pirates' Adventure Castle Activity Centre on our very first date. I can't believe it. What's wrong with you? Would you take a black person to the Museum of Slavery?† Was this your idea of a joke? The Pirates' Adventure Castle Activity Centre indeed, Stewart Lee. And me standing there, looking at childish mural of a one-legged, one-eyed man stealing treasure. It made me feel incredibly self-conscious about my wooden leg, my eye patch and my pocket stuffed with stolen doubloons. The Pirates' Adventure Castle Activity Centre, my foot.'‡

OK, now normally people would come in faster on that. There was a . . . There was a pause, wasn't there? And then some people down here, and then nothing here, and then after a few seconds some other people, er . . . laughed. Now, we, we, this is for . . . I'm recording this for, er, a DVD release tonight and I would, I would appreciate it if you'd all just start to concentrate a bit more and try and come in faster on the . . . Try and come in faster on things, 'cause it was . . . OK? There's people down here that are

* The McIntyre routine has already gone wrong. Now I am reading from a crumpled piece of paper, which readers of *How I Escaped My Certain Fate* will recognise as my one reliable prop. A proper comedian would not do this.

† If there were black people visible to me in the front few rows, I would always try and look them in the eye at this point so they could see I was not racist, and might perhaps become my friends.

‡ Initially I put this pun in because I thought it was passably amusing, but pretty soon it was clear to me people didn't really think it was worth doing and they politely ignored it. So instead of dropping it, like you would if you were a comedian, I decided to keep it in and do lots more with it.

. . . they're all right, like, here, and then the rest . . .*

Let's have a look at this and see . . . Let's see what it is you're, you're having trouble with here. OK? 'The Pirates' Adventure Castle Activity Centre, my foot.' Yeah? Now, 'my foot', that's a . . . a dismissive figure of speech, isn't it? 'Ooh, my foot.' We've all used that, yeah? OK. But why it's funny here is because . . . in this previous paragraph of the let-ter – and I wrote this, remember, it's not a real . . . it's not a real letter – I've . . . the, the pirate, that's me, he says that he has a wooden leg. Yeah? So, 'my foot', later, that's a callback to that, right? It's a funny . . . It's like something Harry Hill would do. OK? It's not a huge . . . It's not hilarious, right, but normally I would expect more than just a pocket of people and then a delayed reaction around the room for it, OK?† And the worry for me about this, and it should be a

---

* I chose to make the failure of the joke part of the general process of lowering my status throughout the show, as if I felt the audience were at fault for not appreciating my genius. I assume that the punt-ers are joining in with this conceit, and on a good night the audience en masse sort of play the part of an angry crowd that didn't get the joke and allow me to harangue them, rather than an audience that ignored it. Usually they seemed to enjoy this bit of role play.

† The audience laugh here because they enjoy being patronised by a comedian so arrogant as to assume that the failure of the mate-rial can only be the audience's fault, because he believes, or has to believe out of desperation, that he is good at his job. This is an example of me grappling with the conundrum that clowning, essentially, is the struggle of a man attempting to maintain his dig-nity, while contemporary stand-up, increasingly, seems to be about asserting genuine high status – put-downs delivered from above by men in costly threads. Of course, occasionally punters missed the point. A man posted online after a Guildford show that the reason he wasn't laughing at the 'my foot' joke was because he got it but he simply didn't think it was funny, and that therefore I was an idiot to go on about it for so long afterwards.

worry for you as well, is that this bit, the pirate's letter, this is like the fun bit at the top of the show. OK? This show is about eighty, ninety minutes long. The last forty-five minutes of it, you know, is hard going. Neither I nor many critics have even been able to work out if it's supposed to be funny. It's hard. And the, and the . . . and the worry for me is, if you're not going for this, the funny, the funny letter, you know, that's looking like an arid section of . . . So just try and . . . There are people here that are . . . they're coming in fast, you know? You can listen. I don't, I'm not annoyed with you. I don't want to get off on the wrong . . . You know, I really appreciate so many people coming, but I do think . . . This is the biggest crowd I've done in Glasgow, and I think it has, necessarily, it's thinned it out a bit, in terms of the, you know . . . This is the old crowd that would come and see me, here, they're operating fast. The rest of you are like, 'What, you know, what's this supposed to be?' And I, I'm . . .*

It's sort of . . . Look . . . You have my sympathy, you know? It's, it's 2010, it's a weird time to be . . . for stand-up. You know? It's a weird old time. 'Cause you, you sit at

* The nice thing about the whole failed 'my foot' joke riff here, though, is it allows me to warn the audience that there is weird stuff ahead. I'm letting them know it doesn't matter if they don't think it's funny. In one sense, the big crowds I play now are easier than the small crowds I was working with for the shows detailed in *How I Escaped* . . . It's statistically more likely that someone will be laughing, and you can start with just one person and build to most of the room. Famous comedians can forget this. Many of the acts you see storming big stages would die in the small clubs where they started out, the slack patches in their material mercilessly exposed in close-up, their muscle gone to fat. (I don't include myself here. I used to die in the small clubs on the way up anyway. I was never a bankable act. I am fat, though.)

home, don't you, all of you, watching Michael McIntyre on the television, spoon-feeding you his warm diarrhoea. You know . . . I'm not going to be doing that. You know? I haven't noticed anything about your lives. They're not of interest to me. This is a letter from a pirate. It's not about going to the shops or anything.

OK? There isn't going to be time to go over everything in this level of detail. So just try and . . . OK. Well, I'll just finish this bit, and then we'll . . . There's only, like, another little bit of it. I'll finish this, and then we'll get back to the, er, the coffee bit.*

[*reading from piece of paper*] 'The Pirates' Adventure Castle Activity Centre, my foot,' er . . . Yeah, it doesn't matter now.† 'As a pirate, I have spent my whole professional

---

* Again, I enjoyed breaking down the illusion, carefully maintained by most comics, that punters are watching a spontaneously occurring thought process, by explicitly telling them that the show had a structure which I was trying to maintain in the face of mounting chaos and lack of audience co-operation. Ironically, by randomly skewering the show's apparent opening through-line with unpredictable smoke and faltering interaction with the crowd, I probably ended up creating a more genuinely spontaneous spectacle. At the Cheltenham Jazz Festival in 2010, the drip-drip of a leaky theatre roof threatened to overwhelm a delicate piece of improvisation by the saxophonist Evan Parker and the trumpeter Peter Evans. When a stagehand actually amplified the drips by coming onstage and placing an echoing metal bucket under the leak, the musicians had no option but to play with the pulse and timbre of the drips, leading, in the end, to sustained applause from an audience that realised they had seen an unrepeatable moment. I suppose what I have been trying to do in this show so far is coerce a similar situation into being, a process that shall henceforth be known by comedians and musicians as Parker's Drip.
† Returning, pointlessly, to the flawed 'my foot' pun, it finally gets a massive laugh, despite being of little value, for the sheer audacity

life climbing rigging, sliding down masts and jumping into pools of blue plastic balls. Er . . . And I have no desire to continue to do this in my spare time. Shiver me timbers. Yours, B. Beard.'

[*Stew gestures to pocket of laughter in front row, then shrugs and grabs his ear as if to tell the rest of the audience to get their act together and listen. He folds up the piece of paper and puts it back in his pocket.*]

That's finished now.*

Second thing that I like . . . Blackbeard, isn't it? . . . The second thing that I like about the Caffè Nehru is the Caffè Nero loyalty card.† Er, there are nine little stamps on

---

of trying it again. If repeated with enough confidence, apparent defeats can become little victories. This notion is, I suspect, derived from my exposure to the free improviser Derek Bailey. Upon accidentally walking into the back wall of the Royal Festival Hall during a concert I saw there in 1997 and getting an unexpected clang out of his guitar, Bailey then carefully repeated the action, incorporating it into the ongoing flow of ideas, as if daring the audience to find fault with it.

* A whole collision of little moments which never existed on the page and evolved live, as I find myself working towards an ideal of unwritable stand-up. The crappy 'B. Beard' joke, as poor as the 'my foot' one, is appended to the end of the letter, swiftly swept over, and then returned to as an aside at the start of the next section. It's the exact same technique as the 'my foot' slight return, but done in four seconds, not four minutes.

† Each night, for my own amusement, I would try to pronounce 'Caffè Nero' in as many different ways as possible. On some level this may be a subconscious parody of how faux-sophisticates pronounce anglicised foreign brand names, but really it was just a silly bit of fun derived, I suspect, from the actor Kevin Eldon. Kevin is a slave to a strange verbal tick whereby he pronounces, for example, the phrase '**Star** Trek' (where any normal person would place the emphasis on the first syllable) as '*Star* **Trek**' (perversely weighting

here. It is full. Right? But when, er, I presented this at the Caffè Nero in Oxford Street in London last year, er, it was rejected, and I wonder if . . . wonder if you can see why that might have been, er, rejected, sir?

[*Stew leans down to front row. Audience member #1 studies card.*]

Normally it's just quick, this bit.*

---

instead the second syllable). Richard Herring and I absorbed this by osmosis on our mid-nineties Radio 1 show, leading to weekly mis-emphasis of the phrase '**Broad**casting House' as 'Broad**cast**ing House.' I still use what is known in the trade as Eldon's Wrong Em**pha**sis (with the stress on the syllable 'pha') onstage at random moments all the time.

* I pretty much always said, 'Normally it's quick, this bit,' at this point, as it seemed to ensure that the punter would become flustered and the simple act of recognising that there were two colours of stamp on the loyalty card would become a long-drawn-out process. It also took the pressure to deliver any entertainment off – the audience had already been told that what was happening wasn't supposed to be enjoyable or a real part of the show, which meant they could relax into it and then find it funny for what it was, instead of what it wasn't. I think this is called neurolinguistic programming, and it has been popularised in entertainment by Derren Brown, whom I hereby allow to call himself 'The Stewart Lee of Magic'.

There were infinite ways this interaction with the punters could go wrong, or be forced to go wrong, and I was, as I intended, kept on my toes by this bit every night for months. In Leicester I began berating a woman in the front row for not recognising the two colours on the card I had given her, when she politely explained that she was registered blind, causing a sharp intake of breath from the audience. It's the sort of moment stand-ups sometimes don't recover from. Once, at a gig on *The Tattershall Castle* boat on the Thames hosted by a young Michael McIntyre, I was trying a new bit in which I maintained that putting flowers at the roadside where there had been motoring fatalities was my idea, and that as I had done it first anyone else doing so should pay me. I then described harassing grieving people, in the act of placing their bouquets, for money. It wasn't going brilliantly, as I was as yet unsure of what the point of it was, but the death of the piece was ensured when a man in the audience shouted out, 'My brother just died in a car crash, fat boy!' before storming out. I abandoned the bit and chose instead to discuss how individual experiences can alter a room's response. It was interesting, but not especially funny. Afterwards, some people came up and said the man's brother hadn't died, but that he had disliked me and had thought that shouting out that comment would ruin the act, which it did. Oddly, I had been confronted at the same venue a few years previously by a woman objecting to my Lady Di bit on personal grounds too. They seem to take things especially personally at *The Tattershall Castle*.

Trying to address the supposedly grieving man's concerns rationally was a mistake. Confronted with a situation like this, the boldest course of action is to try and make things worse. We'll never really know, underneath the rumour and journalistic sensationalism, what happened when Frankie Boyle, after making a joke about the dress sense of Down's syndrome kids, was confronted from the floor by the distressed mother of a Down's syndrome kid who, by her own online admission, had been enjoying the show up to that point, loved Frankie's 'politically incorrect' humour and found him personally arousing. Boyle tried to explain himself, and that he didn't give a fuck, as he was giving up stand-up soon anyway. But in order to stay in character as the man who says the unsayable, Boyle should really have then moved on to saying he would like to kill the woman's child, and all her family, irrespective of any medical conditions they may have, which I believe he did not. Perhaps the whole situation might then have transcended itself.

In 1990 I remember being on a bill organised by the left-wing collective CAST in a library in Kensal Green, and typically the bussed-in audience consisted mainly of people in wheelchairs, many with obvious mental problems. One wheelchair-bound young man, clearly relieved permanently of whatever conscious barriers inhibit most of us, began shouting inappropriate and explicit sexual requests at the comedienne Judy Pascoe, principally concerning his desire to view her reproductive organs and gain access to her breasts. Judy was a refugee from the Australian daredevil troupe Circus Oz whom I had seen hanging upside down from the roof of the Assembly Rooms in 1987, and she was now doing stand-up, but she bit the bullet and abandoned any squeamishness to reply to the man's comments with unbridled force, pouring cold water on his hopes of tupping her. (Libertarians would argue that political correctness actually patronises minorities by protecting them from the personal abuse the rest of us face all the time, and against my better judgement I would imagine on some level it was exhilarating for the shouting man in the wheelchair to be taken seriously as a threat by Ms Pascoe.)

In a similar situation in a pub in Chiswick in 1992 I saw the fiery circuit legend Ian Cognito mistake the persistent interruptions of a Tourette's sufferer in a wheelchair, on a night out with his carers, for malicious heckling and come down hard on the guy, to the obvious discomfort of the audience, who could see what Ian, blinded by the lights, could not. But Ian soon realised what had happened. His stage persona is of a disaffected and jaded psychopath whom the vile blows and buffets of life have so incensed that he is reckless in what he does to spite the world. It wouldn't make dramatic sense for Ian Cognito to back down. Thinking on his feet, Cognito made the shouting, shaking man the focus of his act for the rest of the set, blaming him for interrupting, defusing the situation, creating a bizarrely heart-warming vibe and quite honestly making the man's day. He judged it perfectly, in the moment, in a way a genuinely heartless turn just couldn't have. If you're pretending not to care, you really have to care on some level. If you actually don't care, then I suppose you just don't care.

We rejoin our tale as I have just attacked a blind woman, in front of a thousand Leicestershire people, for not being able to see. Perhaps remembering Ian's approach, which has become known in the trade as Cognito's Relentless Unforgiving Spastic Assault, I blamed the woman for sitting near the front and sabotaging an already problematic evening, and raged at her for making me look like some kind of Frankie Boyle comedian of hate. After a few minutes of this the audience came round. I have since seen the woman many times around the country after gigs, and we always have a good laugh about the incident. She, however, has not seen me.

AUDIENCE MEMBER #1: No.

No. You handed it back. You know what? I've done this 120 times, this show. Sometimes people have struggled, but no one's ever just given up immediately. Look at it again, you lazy man.

AUDIENCE MEMBER #2: It's not stamped.

Huh? It is stamped.

AUDIENCE MEMBER #2: It's not stamped.

What . . . It is stamped. I told you, there's nine stamps on it. It isn't meant to be like a . . .

AUDIENCE MEMBER #2: Couple of faded stamps there.

They're not faded.

AUDIENCE MEMBER #2: That's not stamped.

It is stamped. This has never, ever taken this long. And it would be the night it's . . .

AUDIENCE MEMBER #2: There's seven stamps there.

There's not seven stamps on it. [*lies flat at the front of the stage to continue the discussion*] Right, look. Normally, I just hand this down immediately . . .

AUDIENCE MEMBER #2: I'll accept they . . .

What are they? Look. What's that there?

AUDIENCE MEMBER #2: That's not a stamp.

It is a stamp.

AUDIENCE MEMBER #2: That's, that's seven stamps.

It's seven red ones, and what colour are those?

AUDIENCE MEMBER #2: That's just not even a stamp.

It is a stamp!

AUDIENCE MEMBER #2: That's a blank space.

That's a blue stamp!

AUDIENCE MEMBER #2: No, that's . . . Aye, a blue stamp on a blue background.

Yeah, it doesn't matter what colour background it's on. It's still a stamp.

AUDIENCE MEMBER #2: There's no stamps there.*

There are stamps there. Look. I wouldn't have given this to you if it was wrong, would I? This obviously leads into the rest of what I'm trying to talk about. So I wouldn't have handed you something that didn't support the following hour of the show.

AUDIENCE MEMBER #2: The problem was you didn't get your, er, free coffee because you only had seven stamps.

No, I got . . . This is, this is just appalling. This is my one chance, mate, to film this, and you've . . .

AUDIENCE MEMBER #2: You're two stamps short of a coffee.†

No, I'm not. No, I'm not. There, it's 'cause they're blue.

AUDIENCE MEMBER #2: On a blue background.

Yeah, it doesn't matter what colour background they're on . . .

AUDIENCE MEMBER #2: You've got a nice 'N' shape here with the . . . but that's it.

Doesn't matter what shape it's in! It's just . . .

AUDIENCE MEMBER #2: There's no stamp there. There's no ink.

---

* This, the night of the recording of the DVD of the show, was quite honestly the longest this process has ever taken. I couldn't have been happier, and I knew it was going to make for a unique bit of film, a stand-up genuinely struggling for minutes on end over the most basic piece of set-up. Credit must go here to the Glasgow audience too, who have a superb attitude to stand-up, or at least the ones who come to see me do. They heckle and harass you, but only, in my experience, as far as they think you can handle it. They're like a cat playing with a mouse. They want you to suffer, and to be afraid, but they also want to keep you alive, to prolong their pleasure in your pain.

† It is rare that the public are genuinely funny. This man is an exception, and we were so lucky he sat where he did. What a genius.

There is. There's blue ink there.

AUDIENCE MEMBER #2: There's no blue . . . There's blue ink on a blue background.

Yeah, but you just said there wasn't any ink and then you said there's blue ink on a blue background.

AUDIENCE MEMBER #2: Yeah, but I don't, I don't know what colour that . . . the background was before you stamped it.

It was . . . It was blue!

AUDIENCE MEMBER #2: You've got a blue background, you've got seven reds, you've got two blanks.

They're blue, they're not blank! They're blue!

AUDIENCE MEMBER #2: As far as I'm concerned you're another couple of Americanos short.*

God! [*gets to his feet*] Look, what normally happens, right, is that I just pass this down, anywhere else in the country, apart from Glasgow, where I *chose to film this*, I just give this to someone in the front row. They go, 'Oh, there's seven red, two blue.' This man's got into a, a metaphysical debate about how the blue ink doesn't count 'cause it's on a blue background. It doesn't matter! There's two . . . And now what's happened is the whole room is suspicious and doubts this. This isn't supposed to be a big deal! It's just a bit of fun at the top! If he's doing his best, I think he . . . The problem is now, everyone's going, 'Oh, I don't . . .'†

Look, here's an enlarged one, right? Can you see?

---

* Don't milk it! Here, the genius Glaswegian has got carried away, tried to be funny a second time, and blown it. Professional stand-ups may make comedy look easy, but it is actually quite hard.

† Whatever happened in the room I had to use it to get to this point of exasperation before pulling out a clearly pre-prepared prop.

[*produces enlarged Caffè Nero loyalty card from jacket pocket*] Still a terrible doubt amongst the Glasgow sceptics. Look, this is as big as my scanner goes. [*produces an even larger loyalty card from the wings*] Can you now see? Can you see now that there's two . . .

AUDIENCE MEMBER #2: That's two blues there.

Yeah. They're blue, yeah. Look . . . What I've done, just 'cause . . . I've done a painting of it, right? [*goes to wings and produces even larger Caffè Nero loyalty card, crudely painted*] Now . . . now this was rejected by the Caffè Nero. Not this. This wasn't rejected. I didn't go in with this and go, 'Can I have a free coffee? I've got this . . .' This wasn't rejected. This [*small card*] was rejected. But this is basically, it's the same. Just I've done it bigger.*

* The reveal of the props, culminating in the massive Nero card, is couched as a response to the audience's failure to read the card clearly, but the pre-prepared nature of the massive cards presumably tips them off en masse that my apparent failure to get what I wanted out of them was actually being stage-managed all along as a set-up to this gag. Last year, after I'd laid this show to rest, I read a biography of W. C. Fields (*Man on the Flying Trapeze* by Simon Louvish [Faber and Faber]), who spent the late nineteenth and early twentieth centuries touring the variety stages of the world as a comedy juggler. His show-stopping act was juggling cups. Having got the cups into an impressive tower on his hand, he would take the applause for this incredible feat and then take a bow, letting the cups fall forwards, whereupon they stayed in their formation, thus revealing they had been pre-secured in place. This double bluff, from over a century ago, is the juggling equivalent of everything this stand-up set has been working towards at this point. There is nothing new.

What's strange is that even though the device of revealing the pre-prepared prop made explicit that my apparent failure to do funny material or engage with individual audience members was carefully micromanaged, it did not prevent people feeling that

Now the problem seemed to be, from what I could work out, that, er, the first three 'N's there are red, 'N's one through three. Er, the second two 'N's, 'N's four and five, despite a lot of hostility here, er, are blue. Er, and the last four 'N's, 'N's six through nine there, are . . .

[*Stew scrapes the mic across 'N's six through nine. Audience laughs. As though baffled, Stew does it again.*]*

I might actually be a genuinely incompetent comedian. John R. Finan, having seen the DVD recommended by Dara Ò Briain, pasted this doubtful review onto Amazon:

> Stewart Lee seems to put together A and B and C in unexpected ways. This means comedians might find it funny. But the general public would find [it] utterly unfunny. To give an analogy; Picasso could actually paint really really well. Almost photographic quality. It was only when he broke all the 'rules' of painting that he became famous though. And people said he was a genius. But if all you saw was his messed up paintings of women with a nose where their ear should be, you could be forgiven for saying 'This guy can't paint. Why is he famous?' Stewart Lee, I think, might be the Picasso of comics. He didn't make me laugh. But professional comics can probably appreciate it, and laugh or whatever. Of course, that could all be rubbish. Maybe he's hilarious and I just don't get it. But I don't personally see much difference between a guy who studiously and ironically pretends not to be funny and pretends to have a comedic routine fall apart on stage and pretends to restart the show . . . and a guy who simply is not funny and who's comedic routine falls apart and has to restart the show.

* Again, the fact that this scraping sound was funny was discovered onstage, not pre-written. With much trial and error I eventually managed to make the scraping sound funny every night. Believe it or not, some scrapes are funny and some aren't. I wonder what TV commissioners, who go through scripts trying to work out if the words on them might be funny when said by actors, would make of that. It's almost as if the menu is not the same thing as the meal.

What's going on there, then? That funny, is it, the scraping? In front of a Glasgow audience who sat stony-faced through the 'my foot, wooden leg' callback. 'We went to the Citizens . . . We went to the Citizens Theatre on Monday in the, in the comedy festival, and this . . . a man, a man came out at the start, and it was dreadful. There are all these words and you're supposed to listen to them, and colours you were supposed to identify. It was awful, we were going to go. But then, after about ten minutes, he scraped a microphone stand on a bit of old card. Oh, it was marvellous. It was like something Harry Lauder would've done in the same venue a thousand years ago.'

The problem seemed to be, Glasgow, that these two were blue, and the suspicion was that I'd, that I'd faked them. The, the, the implication being – let's think about this, follow it through – that I'd harvested the first four 'N's, the first three 'N's, harvested the first three 'N's through the normal, er, Caffè Nero purchase-and-reward procedure, then I'd become impatient, and I'd thought, 'I don't think I can wait for my heavily discounted coffee.' So I'd gone away, got a little courgette or bit of okra or something . . . or a chip, like *you* would use . . . and I'd . . . carved a tiny 'N' into the top of it, stamped out two of my own 'N's, unbeknownst to me in an inadmissible colour, and then lost my nerve, lost my taste for crime and thought, 'Ooh,

_____

The trick to making the scrape funny was to do it as if it were incidental to the gesture of pointing out the 'N's and feel myself surprised by the laugh, rather than to try and force the joke, as Bill Murray does in *Groundhog Day*, running breathlessly towards the same funny moments, which he knows are coming, in his nightly effort to woo Andie McDowell. Eventually, the scraping became a big part of the show, tied back into all the 'my foot' stuff from earlier, which hadn't really worked the first or second time around.

no. Stealing two-ninths of a cup of coffee, that's enough for me. I'm not a career criminal.'* So I'd gone away and I'd gathered the final four 'N's [*scrape*] there through the . . . Ha ha!† You like that, do you? The scrape. D'you know what? I probably won't be able to give you the show you want. I'll put extra scraping in.

* Reading this bit back, though it never occurred to me at the time, it seems to parallel the 2008 show *Rhod Gilbert and the Award-Winning Mince Pie* by Rhod Gilbert, who once let me sleep a night in one of his many houses and who, like Mark Watson, is another of Wales's top comedians. I'd seen Rhod's show, and it elevated that sort of mainstream 'annoyance at everyday things' shtick to theatrical or literary levels of hysteria, paranoia and absurdity that observational stand-up rarely approaches, whilst also smoothing seamlessly Rhod's path towards the mainstream. The conceit of the show was that Rhod was fed up of being described as 'surreal' and was therefore going to try and connect with ordinary people by writing about the real world, in all its infuriating banality. Critics and awards panellists liked this notion as it suggested that they were being listened to, but the conceit also enabled Rhod to do more accessible material but with a sort of arch and ironic distance. Old fans would appreciate the comic notion that these concessions to popular taste were being made reluctantly; new fans wouldn't even notice that anything unusual was happening. Reading this set again now, it may be that, subconsciously, seeing Rhod's show suggested to me the idea that I could do more mainstream material if there was a framing device that suggested I was in some way doing it against my better judgement. Rhod's stand-up output, meanwhile, seems to have slowed down of late. I expect it is time-consuming driving around the country hoping that exasperating things happen to you. It is much easier simply to go on and on about the same thing for ages, as I do.
† Here I bashed the first three 'N's with the microphone and then, with a flick of the wrist, turned the 'biff' of the fourth bash into the slightest, briefest scrape. Which somehow always got a laugh. Again, the funniness of the scrape here was discovered by accident, and then ruthlessly replicated night after night.

I, I was annoyed with the *barista* at Caffè Nehru, 'cause the implication was not only that I was fraudulent but also that I was cowardly and sort of lacked the resolve to see the crime through. And I was embarrassed as well, and this probably sounds like the ramblings of a sort of egomaniac, but this was June last year and in, in April, March last year I did a telly thing for BBC2, and it was the first bit of telly I'd done for over a decade, and I was just worried that someone in the queue was going to recognise me and go, 'Ooh, look, there's that bloke off the telly. There's that bloke off the telly trying to steal two-ninths of a cup of coffee.'*

But as it happened, I needn't have worried, 'cause the viewing figures were actually so low that I was less likely to be recognised as me than I was to hear someone go, 'Oh, look, Terry Christian's let himself go.' 'Oh, look, Morrissey's let himself go.' 'Oh, look, Edwyn Collins has let himself go.' 'Oh, look, Ray Liotta's let himself go.' 'Oh, look, Todd Carty's let himself go.' 'Oh, look, Leonardo DiCaprio's let himself go.' 'Oh, look, k. d. lang's let himself go.' 'Oh, look, Hattie Jacques has let himself go.' 'Oh, look, the lead singer of UB40's let himself go.' 'Oh, look, a nineteen-thirties newspaper cartoon of Tarzan's face has let himself go.'†

* Twitter and the blogosphere have made being an E-list celebrity an especially paranoia-inducing affair. Still, if I ever forget exactly what I was talking to my son about on the bus every morning, I can always Google the many sites where people have seen fit to share our private conversations with their readership. That said, being an E-list celebrity also got me the money for a mortgage.

† All these faces are faces my face has at some point been compared to. This bit is a composite of years of similar bits. The Tarzan face idea was mine. The Hattie Jacques comparison comes from my live promoter, John Mackay, who subsequently supplied me with a framed picture of my face next to Hattie Jacques's to prove his point. It now hangs in my toilet, positioned at such a

So in the end I lost my temper with the *barista* at Caffè Nehru. And I said to her the first thing that came into my middle-aged, middle-class, liberal, broadsheet-newspaper-reading mind. I said to her, 'This is absolute nonsense.' I said to her, 'Quite frankly, this is absolute corporate . . . flimflam.' Then I stormed out of the Caffè Nero.

I say 'stormed out'. I was pushing a pram, right. I stormed as far as the door, and I tried to sort of wedge that, and an old lady went, 'Can I help you?' And I went, 'Well, I'm storming out.' And she said, 'It is stormy, isn't it, for June?' And I stormed past her, I stormed along the street for about four hundred yards, and then I remembered that I'd left the milk warming up in the microwave at the Caffè Nero.*

Now, you can't storm out of somewhere in a rage against the corporate homogenisation of the high street and then immediately go back in, pleading for milk. So, um, what I did, Glasgow, I waited about thirty minutes, and then I went back in. And I went, 'Hello.' And she went, 'Yeah?' I went, 'It's me.' And she went, 'Ooh, the false "N" man.' And I went, 'Well, that was . . . I didn't do that, it was one of your, you know, other shops.' And she went, 'What?' And I went, 'Well, er, ha ha, you've got my milk.' And she went, 'Well, it's gone cold now.' And I went, 'Yeah, you know, can I have it back?' And I . . . I thought, 'I can't do it here, it would be embarrassing.' So I went over the . . . I went over the road to a . . . there's a Starbucks opposite there, on the Soho Square, I went in there and I said, 'Ooh, this

---

height that it is often splashed with piss.

* The fun in this bit, for me, comes from trying to perform a Michael McIntyre-style observational bit, but with a percolating subtext of late-period Rob Newman-style anti-corporate anarcho-punk paranoia.

has happened, you know.' And they went, 'Well, yeah, you know, have some . . .' They gave me some . . . boiled water and I went in the . . . I went in the toilet there and I . . .*

Basically, if you remember, what happened was I went in the . . . [*produces loyalty card from top pocket*] in the Caffè Nero. Yeah? And there was, er . . . an, an altercation involving the loyalty card. And I thought, 'Ooh, I could write a routine about that.'† That's the kind of thing you like now, isn't it? I've seen it on *Live at the Apollo*, all stuff about going to the shops. [*puts loyalty card back in top pocket*] Just, I . . . I couldn't really think of an end for it.‡

---

* This bit worked best if I could genuinely forget, nightly, what I was trying to say and how I was trying to say it. In each show, I tried to paint myself into a corner and throw the gig. In the early nineties I saw the avant-guitarist Fred Frith trying to begin an improvisation at the ICA. Distracted by photographers, he told them he was trying to forget where he was and they kept reminding him. I too was involved in an ongoing process of forgetting. I made this same point in my last book, using the same example, but I am involved in an ongoing process of forgetting, as I believe I mentioned. Did I? Did I say that already?

† Here the two threads of this whole section come together in the phrase 'Ooh, I could write a routine about that,' namely the notion that the observational routine is in some way ironic, and yet has also been generated through the normal experiential processes that would lead to the fermentation of an observational comedy routine. Imagine a cake. Now imagine having that cake, but somehow also eating it at the same time. Are you imagining it? Good. Well, that's what I've done in this bit, yeah?

‡ There was usually a big laugh here for the sheer audacity of pissing away the whole opening section of the show with the words 'I couldn't really think of an end for it.' But the laugh also comes, I think, from the shared realisation between performer and audience that such a routine probably isn't even worthy of being finished. Did something amusing happen to you in a shop? Who cares?

Look, I'm . . . I'm forty-one. Right? I've been doing this . . . twenty-odd years now. I can't just . . . I can't just change to what's . . . 'We all do that,' you know. I don't know how to do that. I can't. I'm forty-one, and about five months ago I read an interview with the thirty-eight-year-old comedian Frankie Boyle, and he said that no one over forty should do stand-up. He said [*produces piece of paper from jacket pocket and unfolds it*], 'Most comedians are rubbish once they hit forty and their focus and anger really goes.'

[*Stew folds up piece of paper and puts it back in his pocket. Wanders disconsolately about the stage. Suddenly, he picks up the giant Caffè Nero loyalty-card painting and starts raging.*]

Look at that! Look at the rage in the brush strokes! Look at it! That's the work of a furious man. Look! I was absolutely livid when I painted this . . . satirical attack on an administrative error in the Caffè Nero loyalty-card system. Look at it! Look! Has Frankie Boyle got a painting?! Of a Caffè Nero loyalty card?! That he's done himself?! That he takes around all his thirty-grand corporate gigs, waving in the face of the management of Tesco's?! At Christmas?!* [*throws the painting to the floor in despair and kicks it*] Look at this. You can see where he's coming from.

[*Angrily, Stew rips the painting in half.*]†

---

* I got through a number of giant loyalty-card paintings on the tour as they bend and break, and I'd use poster paints to remake them. The trick was to make the card look as if someone with no artistic talent had done their very best to do the painting as well as possible. I had to look as if I was really trying to do the routine, and the painting, properly. If the cards were too good, or too self-consciously shoddy, they weren't as funny. If I layered the paint on in thick globs, it also provided a good, sonorous surface for the mic scrape.

† I rarely ripped the painting up like this, but it was the last night

AUDIENCE: Ooh . . .

Yeah, fuckin' . . .

He's thirty-eight years old. He's a young, young man. He's still got the rage. Frankie Boyle, he's got the anger, he's got the righteous fury of youth on his side. And I envy him.*

Frankie Boyle, I envy him . . . I saw him on this programme, he's furious. I don't know what it's called, the programme. All the angry young comics are on it. And I'm not on it. There's a microphone stand in the middle of a ring and they all . . . they run towards it. And the angriest one gets there first. I don't know what it's called. There's Frankie Boyle, there's another one, he's old, he's got a moustache and he's bald, he's like a musketeer. Or a Spanish nobleman. A highwayman. There's a little young one, someone's nephew, I think. He's just happy to be there. He thinks it's magical. Blinking away in the lights.† And they're all furious, and Frankie Boyle's the angriest. And when I saw it, he was the angriest one on it. And he,

---

of the tour. The audience seemed genuinely upset at seeing the destruction of something that someone has, however badly, made themselves.

* I suppose what I am noting here is the way that 'anger' and 'angry' have become a kind of critical shorthand for a certain type of comic in journo-speak, usually someone who shouts and/or displays a degree of hostility to often quite blameless figures. In saying I 'envy' Boyle, I'm creating a character for myself as a bitter, jealous man, a man I could so easily be, which allows me a certain leeway as the show progresses.

† This is a classic satirical trick, to describe something commonplace and familiar, here the television comedy quiz Mock the Weak, as if it were alien and strange. Hopefully, it also makes Mock the Weak's standard modus operandi of fabricated anger in fake improv set-ups seem a little absurd.

he ran . . . towards the microphone stand. The others went, 'Oh, go on . . .' [*mimes*] They're about to speak, you know, but then they realise that he's the most angry and they let him go. He got to the microphone stand, I don't know if you saw it, and on this occasion he was angry about the Queen's vagina . . . Frankie Boyle. He was absolutely furious about the Queen's vagina.* He was red in the face with rage about it. I thought he was going to have a heart attack. Particularly, it was particularly about how old it was, this had irked him. Particularly the age of the Queen's vagina pushed old Frankie Boyle off the edge and into a frenzy. But through the red mist Frankie Boyle, he was able to speculate that the Queen's vagina was so old that it would be haunted, and he had . . . this had annoyed him especially. The fact that the Queen's vagina would be haunted had made Frankie Boyle insane with hate.

Now I'm by no means an expert on the supernatural, but my understanding of hauntings is that the age of a structure is immaterial and that they're most likely to occur at the scene of a terrible tragedy.

[*Stew points at the front row for the benefit of the rest of the room.*]†

---

* Through no fault of his own, the journalistic tag for Boyle is that he is 'angry' or 'the angry man of comedy'. I've never seen him live, but he and his team of writers seem to come up with a lot of rather cleverly constructed jokes, like Jimmy Carr's, in which the excuse of 'anger' is not really relevant or necessary.

Taking Boyle's celebrated 'Queen's old haunted pussy' joke, which so incensed Emily Maitlis on *Newsnight*, neutering it with the application of anatomically precise language and then suggesting that this neat little gag was born in some way out of anger amused me no end, and I struggled each night to maintain the required degree of seriousness and fury as I ranted on about it.

† The implication here is that the Queen's congress with the Duke

That's the best joke in the show. And they were . . . They're still coming in first down here, aren't they? And all the other people are going, 'Ooh, what's that about?' Come on. For the DVD recording. Come on. Team A there [*front row*]. One bloke clapping alone up there [*balcony*]. It's no good, is it? Listen to them, they're . . . Now . . .

No, he was furious, though, about the Queen's vagina, Frankie Boyle. Now, er . . . I'm forty-one, I don't mind about the Queen's vagina. At my age, if I think about the Queen's vagina, I'm at worst ambivalent about it. Eighteen months ago, when I was young, it would've driven me over the edge. I tell you, eighteen months ago, Glasgow, when I was young, if I'd thought about the Queen's vagina, even for just a nanosecond, I would've been so angry that I would happily have punched every single one of you in the face. But not any more. You know? I'm a . . . I'm a forty-one-year-old. I'm old. I'm a forty-something parent of a two-year-old child. I spend most of my time hanging around playgrounds in north-east London with other forty-something parents of young children. We're not angry about the Queen's vagina. Very rarely even comes up.

You know, we're angry about grown-up stuff: we're angry about the collapse of the infrastructure in the inner city, we're angry about the lack of educational provision for our kids in London. A friend of mine, he had a little girl, turned out she was dyslexic, and they were worried about whether she would thrive and prosper in the over-subscribed inner-city London school system. So they, they

---

of Edinburgh and the subsequent birth of her children are the tragedies. Or perhaps some non-specified vaginal event which the audience can imagine themselves. Either way, only a minority of the room would laugh here, which gave me an opportunity to further divide the crowd.

sold up and they . . . they left London and they moved to the countryside, and the, the little girl went to school in the countryside. And she's grown up to be a racist. Who can spell. It's the most dangerous kind.*

I thought about moving to the countryside, though. I've got a two-bedroom flat in, in Hackney. I worked out I could've sold it and got a house somewhere like North Wales or Herefordshire. I saw this house in Herefordshire advertised on the internet. It said it had a garden. I haven't got a garden where I live. It said it had a river running through the garden. I haven't got a river running through the garden, I haven't got a garden. And at the bottom of the page the estate agent had put: 'From the kitchen window you can see otters.' Yeah, otters. That raises the bar, doesn't it?†

* In the end I held onto this bit about schools, and the following section on otters, as a link into the *Top Gear* stuff, but really it belongs in another show, as there's a whole hour or so in these kinds of anxieties, I think. If I were to write a 'parent' set, it would be about how kids force you to engage with the world, crumble your absolutes, compromise your ideals and betray your principles, as they are tested in the field of deeds rather than just left to flourish in an abstract space. I ended up using this in a section on schools in the eventual second series of *Comedy Vehicle*, but I can imagine I might come back to it again one day, as the starting point to a show about children and life choices.

† Online critics complained here about my use of 'animal whimsy', as the otter has become a standard random noun in most, if not all, post-Boosh cutesy surrealist routines. But this piece was based on an advert I saw for a house near Glastonbury which boasted that there were otters in the river in the garden. It's not my fault if Mother Nature chooses to express her bounty in a form that seems clichéd to comedy purists. Why don't you all go to the Otter Trust in Bungay, Suffolk, from where the recovery of Britain's wild otter population was masterminded, and stand at the gates shouting, 'ANIMAL WHIMSY! BORING!'

[*raises an imaginary telephone to his ear*] 'We've got a lovely property you might be interested in, Mr Lee.'

'Hmm. Are there ... [*pause*] visible otters? No? Oh dear. 'Cause if you remember, when I first came in, I did, I did make it very clear to you that, er ... I suffer from a ... an allergy to anything that is not an otter. I suffer from an allergy to all ... all non-otter objects. So, er ... you can imagine how important it is to me to be ... Mm? No, it is real. It's not ... Well, the reason you haven't heard of it is because anyone that has that, they ... they immediately die. This was my, um ... It's very much my last hope. There's only three or four of them there? Well, it's a start, you know, it's a start. Eh? You feel that, um, given that it's an important gig, especially with the sort of messy bit with the card at the beginning, er, it's ill-advised of me to set off at this point on an unplanned improvisation? Yeah, that's very interesting ... that you would think that. There's one bloke really liking it, I don't know if you heard him. No, it's ... It's sort of ... It's going ... I don't know, yeah. I mean, the problem now is it's going sort of ... It's going almost well enough to persist with, but ... If you were me, you'd have got out on the phrase "visible otters"? Yeah, well ... Yes, thank you. Goodbye.'

[*Phone call ends.*]

Now, where I live, otters ... It's ludicrous.* Where I live,

---

* Appear to begin on something else, then double back and whack a capstone on the rambling improv in the shape of the phrase 'Otters ... It's ludicrous.' It's a variation on the comedy technique universally known as Ò Briain's Truncated Appendage, I suppose, where an apparently new phrase is begun before the audience has had time to laugh properly at the completion of the old one. The otters improv started to spread in the last few dates of the tour, but I made myself rein it in for the filming transcribed here. I wanted

in Hackney, in north-east London, from my kitchen window I can see rats, running along the high street, going under the fire station.* The rats are out of control in, er, in most major cities. I'm sure it's the same here. Um . . . Now, there's an old Victorian park where I live, Clissold Park, I walk through it every day. I was walking through it in September and I saw – this is true – I saw a middle-aged, middle-class mum with a little girl about three years old, and the little girl was feeding bread out of a brown paper bag to a mixture of ducks, pigeons and rats, right? There was about eight rats there, running around, going, 'Is this allowed now? Have they changed the, er . . .'† And I said to her, 'What are you doing?' And she said, 'Do you mind? I don't want her to grow up to be afraid of rats.'

We're supposed to be afraid of rats, aren't we? It's deep within our human evolutionary DNA patterns – fear the rats, run away from them so they don't wee Weil's disease into your face. And I wouldn't mind, but there's signs up all round the park saying, 'Please do not feed the pigeons and

---

to try and perform it in series two of *Comedy Vehicle* and didn't want the routine to settle so that it was stale for the TV filming, which is what happened to the Del Boy Falling Through the Bar bit in series one. So the otters improv here is quite truncated. Rest assured, some nights it could go on for hours.

* The first time you see street rats in London, you can't believe it. Then you get used to it. I couldn't handle them in my flat, though. Gareth, over the road, beat one to death in his kitchen. I stopped going running in Finsbury Park after a rat jumped out of bin when I ran past it and scared me. Now I rarely run and my health is suffering. I blame the rats.

† As mentioned before, this story is entirely true, but it happened to my wife, the comedian and woman Bridget Christie. She gave me this, and she took the story of our rubbish Shetland honeymoon for her own stand-up show.

ducks, as it encourages rats.' Now, surely, implicit within that . . . is the suggestion . . . 'Do not feed the rats, as it encourages rats, because they are rats; rats are rats.'

Anyway, I went to look at this otter place in Herefordshire, and it was all right, right, but I thought, 'I'd better go and look at the pub in the village,' 'cause that's all there is to do in the countryside, go to the pub. So I went and looked at the pub in the village in the countryside and I realised I could never live in the countryside because the pub in the village in the countryside was full, exclusively, of middle-aged men dressed from head to toe in supermarket denim who all looked and sounded exactly like Jeremy Clarkson. And I realised I could never live in the countryside, because living in the countryside would be like living in an endless edition of *Top Gear*. And I hate *Top Gear*.*

One bloke cheering, there. Did you hear that? There's one bloke cheering. Yeah, there's one person clapping. There's a little pocket, isn't there, spread across here and here and here, of, like, the liberal *Top Gear* haters. But on

* Prior to the promise of TV money we had been planning to leave London, and this whole *Top Gear* bit, to some extent, represents a creative visualisation of the arguments we had with ourselves, extreme exaggerations of our own anxieties. We fled as young people to urban anonymity. Did we want to go back to a place where everyone knew your name? We saw a house we liked, once, in a Gloucestershire village. The village had a pub, which at least meant there'd be somewhere to sit and drink that wasn't your own kitchen. But the pub was used for BNP celebrations after a half-decent performance in some local election. In London, if your pub becomes a BNP pub you can easily go to another one. But in a village where there is only one pub, you have to make the best of it and try and join in the conversation. 'Evening.' 'Oh, hello. Er . . . hated any new races lately?' 'Yes. Polynesians, actually, and blacks as usual, obviously. Yourself?' 'Oh, you know, just the Jews mainly. You know me.'

the whole, here tonight in Glasgow, probably the majority of the audience are going, 'Well, we like *Top Gear*, it's funny. What's your . . .? Why . . .?'*

The problem is, I hate *Top Gear*. And I hate anyone that likes it. Right? And I'm now, I'm going to explain why that is for about forty-five minutes. OK? And then . . . Then there's a little bit about cider and then that's the end. OK? So you have to try and . . . All right?

OK, now, right. The reason I hate *Top Gear* – and even if you're a *Top Gear* viewer, like most of you are, you have to relate to this – the reason I hate *Top Gear* is 'cause it is wilfully and deliberately politically incorrect, right? And the problem is, I was a student in the nineteen eighties in the kind of era of political correctness, and when I became an Alternative Comedian in the eighties, it was all CND benefits and whatever. So I like political correctness, I think it's good. So I can't relate to *Top Gear*. But I don't think it's aimed at me. Right? It's aimed at a different kind of middle-aged man, isn't it? A kind of frightened middle-aged man in his house, he's scared of how the world's changing, and political correctness has gone mad, and he likes to watch *Top Gear*, don't you? 'Cause it pays . . . it pays no heed to the political correctness or the women's rights or the gays' rights or the true environmental facts.†

---

* Each night I set myself up in opposition to the imagined majority of the room. It was only in conservative towns east and southeast of London that the number of actual *Top Gear* sympathisers caused any real problems, but it was always dramatically useful to cast myself as a brave little hero raging against the hateful mass.

† This 'environmental facts' bit rarely got a big laugh. Sometimes it went to silence. Sometimes it was greeted with outright hostility. The worse this bit went, the better it was for the overall shape of the piece, increasing the jeopardy, ramping up the tension, putting

He likes to watch *Top Gear*, this man. He likes to see Jeremy Clarkson sneer at a Sikh on his behalf. I can't relate to it. I can't relate to it. And that's why you think you like it, isn't it, to go, 'Oh, we like *Top Gear*, it's politically incorrect, it's brilliant.' That isn't why you like it. It's why you think you like it. It isn't. The real reason you like *Top Gear*, the *Top Gear* viewers, the real reason you like *Top Gear*, is because the relationship between the three presenters, Jeremy Clarkson, James May and Richard 'The Hamster' Hammond . . . He's not a real hamster, is he? . . . The reason you like it is because the relationship between the three presenters, er, exactly mirrors the power structure of the relationship of the Three Bears.* And I think you find that very comforting to watch, don't you, *Top Gear* viewers? Richard 'The Hamster' Hammond, he's not a real hamster, he's the baby bear, isn't he? Washing his ears. With his little tiny red shoes he's got on. All shiny buckles all done up.†

---

myself at risk of failure. Accusations that I preach to the converted were often not appropriate in this instance.

* I've a feeling this Three Bears idea wasn't mine, and that it came out of a conversation with someone, but I can't remember who. Do I owe someone money? But once you think of the *Top Gear* power structure – or indeed the relationship of any claque of middle-aged, moaning, prog-rock, anti-PC, car-driving men – in these terms, the illusion of their camaraderie caves in instantly.

† I have three memories of being a toddler, from before I could speak. Coca-Cola fizzed into my nose the first time I ever used a straw, at a metal table overlooking the sea; ice cream dripped on my face as I was propped upright, in my mother's parents' garden, in the shadow of the air-raid shelter; and once I had new, red, buckle-up shoes. We were in the living room at the little terraced house in Northdown Road, and my parents were still together. I can't have been older than three. 'Show Daddy your new shoes,' my mother said. I held up my foot. No one had realised I could understand

And he sits up at the table sometimes, doesn't he, with the others. They let him sit up at the table and he licks up his milk, doesn't he? [*smacks lips, high-pitched baby-bear voice*] 'Lovely milk. I lick up my milk. Lovely, warm, creamy milk . . . From Morrisons.'

Now, Jeremy Clarkson, you probably think he's the father bear, the alpha male, with his outrageous politically incorrect opinions which he has for money.* But he's not! James May is the alpha male in that group, not Jeremy Clarkson. James May – strong, silent. 'Cause you know, if he wanted to, James May could tear Jeremy Clarkson's face off with a single blow of his enormous paw.†

I think the problem I have, as a kind of frustrated, bitter, politically correct, middle-aged liberal, er, is that I can't work out which one of the three *Top Gear* presenters to despise the most. You'd think it would be Jeremy Clarkson, wouldn't you, with his outrageous politically incorrect opinions which he has every week to a deadline in the *Sunday Times*. Almost as if they weren't real. But it isn't, right? 'Cause, you know, I, I . . . the thing about Jeremy Clarkson, right, is I think he's either an idiot or a genius, right. He's either an idiot who actually believes all the badly

───────

what they were saying. There was clapping and applause, and I swear I remember a feeling of personal pride. Perhaps I have spent a lifetime trying to recreate that moment. If I'd held up my new shoes more often, maybe I could have made my parents happy enough to stay together. I suppose it was my fault.

* Clarkson vacillates between saying his opinions are his opinions and, when challenged, trying to suggest that he is in a kind of provocateur role, that he is in character, as if his life is being penned moment to moment by some playful Laurence Sterne character. So do I, I suppose. Imagine a cake, etc.

† Somehow I find it difficult to dislike James May. I don't think he really realises what he's got himself into.

researched, lying, offensive shit that he says. Or he's a genius who's worked out exactly the most accurate way to annoy me. In which case, fair play to him, your . . . your god.*

So it isn't him. The *Top Gear* presenter that I hate the most, and he's someone who I think, on balance, I hate more than anyone who's ever lived, actually, um . . . And it's, er . . . erm . . . Richard 'The Hamster' Hammond, actually. Um. I hate him more than anyone who's ever lived, and, and fictional characters. Like, er . . . Skeletor, if you remember him. No, I hate him. I hate Richard 'The Hamster' Hammond, right, 'cause he's not a real hamster, is he? What he is, he's a man, right, who's been able to carve out a best-selling literary career off the back of his own inability to drive safely. Yeah?

'Cause . . . he had that crash, didn't he, in that dragster, and then he wrote this book about it, *On the Edge*, and it sold millions. And I just think . . . I think there's something a little bit, er, undignified and cynical about all these celebrities writing these cash-in books about some dreadful thing that happens to them, you know? I think there's an, I think there's an, an undignified degree of cynicism in it. Yeah? To the point where I wouldn't be surprised if, when he'd had that crash, Richard Hammond, and he was hanging upside down, waiting to be rescued in that dragster, he wasn't thinking to himself, 'Ooh, I hope I'm quite badly injured in this, then I can do a book about it that'll sell loads.' I'm not saying that he did think that. I'm just saying there does seem to be a, an element of cynicism in it, doesn't there? I wouldn't

* I think Hammond is more interesting than Clarkson and, conveniently, Clarkson bashing has become a bit of a liberal comics' cliché, so it was better to avoid him. Also, as Clarkson's exposed wingman, Hammond is more vulnerable.

be surprised if when he was hanging upside down waiting to be rescued, he wasn't thinking to himself, 'Ooh, I hope I get some brain damage and forget loads of my life. And then on Richard and Judy's Book Club my attractive wife can come on and help me to remember it and it'll create a tender scene.' Look, I'm not saying that he did, he did think that, I'm just saying that there's a degree of cynicism in those books, isn't there? Mm, you know? And what, what's worse, I think, is that that book, *On the Edge*, it's sold millions and it was published through Weidenfeld & Nicolson, and it shouldn't have been. It should've come out through BBC World, the commercial arm of the BBC. Because, you and me, the licence payers, we funded that crash. Yeah? We did. And therefore we are entitled to feel the benefit of any profits derived from it. Yeah? Yeah. And Richard 'The Hamster' Hammond, he knows that. But he went and he wrote that book anyway, and I think it's a cynical thing to do, and I hate him for it, and I wish he'd been killed in that crash.*
Well, I do. I wished he'd been killed and . . . and decapitated, and that the next series of *Top Gear* had been presented by Jeremy Clarkson, James May and Richard Hammond's severed head on a stick. [*walks to the front of the stage*] And if that seems a bit much for all the *Top Gear* viewers . . . it's just a joke, like on *Top Gear*. You know, when they do their jokes, which you like, don't you? 'It's just a joke' – the Jeremy

---

* Just to be clear, I don't wish Richard Hammond had been killed in that crash. However, there is a half-buried and extreme part of me that entertains as true every other aspect of this argument. We live in strange times. When the Pantene-smeared celebrity piano player Myleene Klass and her sleeping child suffered the indignity of a burglary in January 2010, her publicist made sure the story of her valiant, knife-wielding threats to the escaping miscreants made headlines with perhaps indecent haste.

Clarkson defence – 'It's just a joke.' So when I said that I wished Richard Hammond had been decapitated and killed, right, like when they do their jokes on *Top Gear*, it was just a joke. But coincidentally . . . as well as it being a joke, it's also what I wish had happened.* 'Cause I hate Richard 'The Hamster' Hammond. He's not even a real hamster! If he was a real hamster and someone went, 'Do you know, a hamster has survived a 280 mph dragster crash and advertised Morrisons, admittedly with a glazed expression?' you'd go, 'That's a good hamster.' But he isn't a hamster. He's not even a hamster. He's nothing! He's worse than a hamster!

'Cause Jeremy Clarkson, your spiritual king, at least . . . at least he has the guts, doesn't he, to stand there personally expressing his stupid offensive opinions. But Richard 'The Hamster' Hammond doesn't do that, does he? He just stands next to Jeremy Clarkson, giggling. 'Blah, blah, blah, Gypsies.' [*high-pitched, quisling Hammond voice*] 'Ah ha ha ha, Gypsies! Ha ha ha ha ha ha! Imagine being a Gypsy, ah ha ha ha! In a caravan, ah ha ha ha! Aha, not even in a car, aha ha!' 'Blah, blah, lesbians.' [*Hammond voice*] 'Aha, imagine being a lesbian! Ah ha ha ha! Ah ha ha ha ha ha!' 'Blah, blah, the Welsh.' [*Hammond voice*] 'Ah ha ha ha! Ha ha ha! Imagine being Welsh and not being English! Ah ha ha! Ah ha!'

He's nothing! He's like a horrible little shit weasel kid

---

* If I channelled a genuine dislike for *Top Gear* fans and psyched myself up to believe the righteousness of the argument, it was no trouble to stand on the lip of the stage hectoring the often significant percentage of the audience that didn't agree with me, fired up with an exaggerated moral superiority like a crazy street preacher. There was a guy, who looked like Bez, who stood in Oxford Circus for most of the noughties, shouting, 'Are you a sinner or a winner?' at people. I expect he felt much the same.

at school . . . hanging around with all the bullies, laughing at their jokes in the hope they won't pick on him. He's a horrible little shit weasel piece of shit nothing, hanging around with the bullies, laughing at their jokes, licence-payer-funded apologist for institutionalised bullying, and I hate him.*

Picture the scene: the *Top Gear* Christmas night out, Jeremy Clarkson, James May, Richard 'The Hamster' Hammond, he's not a real hamster, they're on the South Bank, two o'clock in the morning, running along the Embankment, drunk. 'Ha ha ha, Gypsies!' And Jeremy Clarkson . . . Jeremy Clarkson sees a homeless man asleep by the river. And that homeless man is probably Scottish, remember. He is, Glasgow. It's one of you that's just having a sleep in the street . . . at Christmas . . . like anyone would. And Jeremy Clarkson sees the Scottish homeless man, and for a joke, to satirise the old loony left, politically correct nutters, he decides to kick him to death. [*mimes repeatedly kicking a tramp*]† So, he's going, [*yells*] 'Come on! Come on, Richard Hammond, kick this tramp to death. Come on!

* It was my live promoter who first described the *Top Gear* team as the school bullies to me, adding that the frustrating thing for him, as a teenage homosexual, was that he was unavoidably attracted sexually to those kinds of boys at school for their power, whilst disliking them in themselves. View the trio in school-bully terms and Hammond's role in proceedings is instantly clarified. Steve Coogan went on to make this point in the same terms in an *Observer* article two years later, but the Twitterverse shepherded readers to my earlier take on the same idea and briefly boosted the DVD of *If You Prefer* . . . to the top of the Amazon charts. Twitter is not all bad.

† Doing this for months on end shattered my right knee, and it's been weak and wobbly ever since. I am not a trained physical theatre performer, and my attempts to branch out into the world of moving around rarely come to much.

It's a joke. Come on! This'll annoy the sour-faced dykes at the *Guardian*. Come on! [*stamping, jumping*] Stamp on the tramp's head, Richard Hammond. This'll annoy Amnesty International. Kick him right up in the guts. Come on, Richard! Kick him to death, Richard Hammond! Come on, this'll upset the grieving relatives of Stephen Gately.'

And Richard Hammond's going, [*squeaky Hammond voice*] 'No, I'll just stand here and film it on my camera phone. Ah ha ha ha! Gypsies! Ha!'*

That's what he is. Nothing. Horrible piece of shit. And you don't need me to tell you this. You know it. You know it. 'Cause there's that famous bit of news footage, isn't there, you can find it on YouTube now, where Jeremy Clarkson and Richard 'The Hamster' Hammond are on some kind of panel in Australia, and Jeremy Clarkson does one of his *Top Gear* jokes. He says that Gordon Brown is a one-eyed Scottish idiot. Now by all means make fun of Gordon Brown's policies, make fun of him being Scottish at a push, if that is amusing to you. But one-eyed?

Right, whatever you think of Gordon Brown, right, he lost his sight as a child, he went blind as a child. And is that a funny thing to do a joke about? He went, he went blind as a child, he's got about 30 per cent vision now, I think, which may be why he didn't cross his 'T's in that letter to that dead serviceman's mother, mightn't it, yeah? Rather than it being a calculated insult to the dead. It

---

* Fat, ill-fed and bleary, the effort of the tramp-kicking mime would invariably leave me breathless and light-headed. I was able to use my physical exhaustion to give the impression of a kind of desperate, emotional sincerity as I recovered from my brief exertions in the following speech. Unable to act on any level, I find the best way to appear exhausted is to be so out of shape that I am able, at the drop of a hat, to become exhausted.

might be the blind . . . I'm not an optician. But if I was the editor of a tabloid newspaper, I would've investigated the blindness. He went, he went blind as a child, and Jeremy Clarkson thinks that is a legitimate . . . I don't know. If you've got, if you've got kids, or any sort of shred of human empathy, why would you . . . If you, you've got kids and they're ill or in hospital . . . every . . . you say to them, 'You'll be all right tomorrow, the next day.' You try and reassure them. And, er . . . But presumably there came a point where . . . Gordon Brown's parents didn't do that any more because he was blind, and that was that, and Jeremy Clarkson thinks that's a funny thing to do a joke about.*

Now, Jeremy Clarkson has three daughters and I hope they all go blind. Not one of them in one eye. All of them in all their eyes. [*shouts*] Come on, it's just a joke like on *Top Gear*! But again, as well as it being a joke . . . No, not really. You wouldn't say that, would you, you wouldn't think it, you wouldn't wish it on a child.†

So he's there, Jeremy Clarkson, on the news, doing his *Top Gear* joke – 'One-eyed Scottish idiot' – and there's Richard Hammond on the clip doing his

* This section is, of course, unabashed emotional manipulation, demagoguery at its worst. But it answers the *Top Gear* gang's bespoke callousness in kind, smothering it in cushions of sentimentality. And to perform it, I thought of my own son, and how I would feel if, as an adult, he was mocked by Jeremy Clarkson for injuries he had sustained as a child. I'm rarely explicitly personal on stage. But in my head, not being an actor, the only way I can give convincing performances of ideas with apparent emotional content is to attach them subconsciously to things that matter to me.

† I make the indefensible joke, and attempt to defend it using glib *Top Gear* logic, to show that the *Top Gear* logic, in and of itself, is not enough.

licence-payer-funded job, laughing away. [*Hammond voice*] 'Ah ha ha ha, blind child, ha ha . . .' But then he realises, Richard Hammond, it's being filmed, you can see it in his brain – click! And maybe this isn't going to play as well as he might imagine at home. So what he does, to try and cover his arse – look at it on the clip – at the same time he's laughing, Richard Hammond tries to make a disapproving face, right? Fighting . . . What he does for about a minute is this. He goes . . . [*Hammond voice*] 'Ah ha ha ha! [*suddenly pensive*] Ah ha ha ha! [*pensive again*] Ah ha ha, blind child, ha . . .' [*pensive*]*

Find that clip, look at it, it's one of the most pitiful things I've ever seen. Look at Richard Hammond's face in that clip, and what you see is the face of a cowardly man trapped between two different forms of cowardice. And I hate him for that. And I wish he'd been killed in that crash. I wish, I wish his head had come off and rolled along the track, and all shards of metal had gone in his eyes and blinded him. 'Cause that's funny, isn't it, on *Top Gear*, going blind. And then I, then I wish his head had rolled into a still-burning pool of motor oil but there was just enough sentience left in his spinal column for him to go, 'Ooh, that's hot,' and then die.†

---

* Look at http://www.youtube.com/watch?v=Qs7V-hnTV3o. All that is required for Jeremy Clarkson to triumph is for Richard Hammond to do nothing.

† In August 2009, when I was running the show in at The Stand, I tried this various different ways, sometimes going further, sometimes softening it, trying to find the right level. It's for this reason that I don't invite the press to the August part of the show-making process. During the last week of the festival I was stopped on the way into the venue by a man from the *Mail on Sunday*. 'Is it right you say you wish Richard Hammond had been decapitated on stage?' I

saw what was happening immediately. The nightmare scenario was that the carefully contextualised bit was shorn of the material that buffered it, an orchestrated boycott ensued and I was forced into a position where, as with *Jerry Springer: The Opera*, I couldn't tour the show, and my ability to earn money for my family was once again compromised. I answered, 'Yes. But it's a joke. Like on *Top Gear*.'

In the end the *Mail on Sunday* ran the story with a picture of Hammond's car blowing up and a transcript of the offending section of the act thus:

Lee spends 20 minutes telling audiences about his dislike of Hammond in his show *If You Prefer A Milder Comedian, Please Ask For One*, at the Edinburgh Fringe Festival, and he incorporates their schooldays into his routine. During one show last week, Lee said: 'I wish he had died in that crash and that he had been decapitated and that his head had rolled off in front of his wife and that a jagged piece of metal debris from the car had got stuck in his eye and blinded him. And then his head had rolled on a few more yards into a pool of boiling oil and that his head had retained just enough neural capacity for him to be able to think "ooh, this is [a] bit hot" before the whole thing exploded into tiny pieces.' Later in the routine, he said: 'I wish Richard Hammond HAD died and I wish he had been decapitated. Of course, it's a joke. But coincidentally it's also what I believe.' Lee said before his Edinburgh show on Friday night: 'I don't want to talk about it. They do jokes on *Top Gear* don't they? Treat it as a joke.'

The violence seemed enjoyably insane out of context, especially mis-transcribed in such clinical language, and the quote has me wishing that Hammond's wife and children had seen his head roll past them, which I don't remember saying. But I may have said this. I did different stuff every night in the try-outs. I don't know. Swiftly the story was all over the tabloids, and was even misrepresented in the *Guardian* and the *Independent* too. I was asked for comment, but declined to clarify any further. I'd learned, from my frustrating experiences trying to defend *Jerry Springer: The Opera* to civic function rooms full of inarticulately furious people up and down the land, that there was simply no point. I looked at the vituperative online comments from hundreds of enraged morons and *Top*

Not really. I don't really think that. Right? And what I was doing there, as everyone here in this room now understands, just in case there's anyone from the *Mail on Sunday* watching this, is I was using an exaggerated form of the rhetoric and the implied values of *Top Gear* to satirise the rhetoric and the implied values of *Top Gear*. And it is a shame to have to break character and explain that. But hopefully it will save you a long, tedious exchange of emails.*

But he is a disappointing figure, isn't he, Richard Hammond, I think. He disappoints me 'cause, you know, you sort of get the sense that he's probably all right really but he's in with a, a bad crowd, you know? And you know what? I should've seen this coming years ago. 'Cause I was actually at school with Richard Hammond.† I was. I was

---

Gear fans, none of whom had seen the show, and waited, hoping it would blow over and that I would not be prevented from working. The mixed ire of *Top Gear* loyalists and *Daily Mail* readers proved an especially toxic mess, many of them expressing the desire that I be banned, though from what was not always clear. One *Mail* reader from Spalding called Sophie wrote: 'I think Stewart Lee should be banned from actually being a so called "comedian".' Fans of human nature will be interested to learn that even when people who had seen the show went on newspaper comment boards to explain the context and purpose of the remarks, the debate continued unchanged. People just want someone to hate.

* This admittedly quite funny coda was appended on the night the *Mail* man stopped me before the show, and in all subsequent shows, so that my intentions were made absolutely explicit and no one trying to stir things up could pretend that they had not explicitly been told the point of the piece.

† I can't remember how I found out Richard Hammond had been at my school. Perhaps it was on Wikipedia. He was actually five years below me. I think I have a slight memory of his tiny young face, but I can't be sure as I never knew him. I went to a private

at a school called, er, Solihull School, in Solihull in the, in the Midlands, in Birmingham. Um, Richard Hammond

---

boys' school in Solihull, Solihull School, funded through it by a part-scholarship, a charity bung from a fund for orphans, waifs and strays, and my mum doing three jobs. I loved it. But this element of the act, in a garbled form, also proved too much for the tabloids to resist. As the *Mail on Sunday* said:

> Lee was at the same school as Hammond – he was two years ahead of the presenter – though the source of the animosity remains unclear. Yesterday, neither of the BBC men were prepared to discuss their days at Solihull School, a public school in Birmingham, amid speculation that their shared school experience may have prompted Lee's diatribe.

Hilariously, the piece closes with the quote: 'His spokeswoman said, "I don't think they knew each other at school."' The *Mail* even dragged the headmaster of my old school, Philip Griffiths, in for comment. (I later wrote him a grateful letter thanking him for the diplomacy with which he handled this, especially given that I remember him finding me quite annoying as a precocious teenager when he taught me history.)

So even though I state onstage that I didn't know Hammond and the piece was made up, the story now was that Hammond and I were both posh public-school boys who had a feud three decades earlier, when in fact, onstage, I went on every night to state explicitly that I never knowingly met him. The *Solihull Observer* was especially banal in its coverage of the story, making the *Mail* look sophisticated in comparison, and kept sending me obsequious emails inviting me to clarify the story, which I declined, so they ran more articles making things seem even worse. Sadly, old friends of my mum read the local paper's lies and, once again, she was quietly embarrassed by the portrayal of me as some kind of sick psychopath. Teenagers wrote to my agent telling her their mums were now forbidding them to go and see me, but I was never actively prevented from performing the show and earning from it, so one has to be grateful for small mercies.

was there. If you don't believe me you can look it up on the Wikipedia, and there's a list there of all the other Z-grade celebrities that went to, to Solihull School. I'm on it. Richard Hammond's on it, he was about five years below me.*

And in the year above me at Solihull School in Solihull in the early nineteen eighties was the original line-up of Napalm Death. And I actually used to go orienteering with Napalm Death. I did, Glasgow. Four Sundays a term, I would go voluntarily to the Brecon Beacons to go orienteering with the original line-up of Napalm Death. But it wasn't square, going-to-the-theatre-and-all-liking-*Top Gear* orienteering, like you would do. It was first-wave, proto-speed-metal, anarcho-punk orienteering. We had maps . . . but all the boundaries were crossed out.

[*to most of audience except front row*] Come on, it's better than . . . it's a better joke. That is the second-best joke in the show. Come on. Follow their lead. Follow them.

And I actually saw the original line-up of Napalm Death do about their third-ever gig, and it was in 1982, and they performed in front of a banner that said, 'PUNK IS A ROTTING CORPSE', at Dorridge village scout hut. But they were nice lads, Napalm Death. Old Nik Napalm, he was the singer. That wasn't his real name, ladies and gentlemen. His real name . . . was Ian Napalm.

---

* The great thing about the fact that Hammond was at my school was that in the telling of the long, made-up story about our schooldays that now follows, I was able, in my mind, to locate the incidents I fabricated in precisely remembered real locations, to almost trick myself that they were real memories. I could cloud the edges of the tale with enough true details so that to me, the teller, the story had the flavour of absolute truth, a flavour usually communicated to the believing audience.

Are you happy now? Is that what you want? That's not what they want. Um, but, er . . . He was a good lad, er . . .*

---

* Three-quarters of The Napalm Deaths (as they were then known) were in the year above me. Solihull School had been a hotbed of punk art in the seventies and eighties, also spawning The Spizzles, Swell Maps, bits of the C86 band Mighty Mighty, *Newsround*'s Lizo Mzimba, LSD guru Brian Cuthbertson and The Throbbing Gristles. Today, the former front man of The Throbbing Gristles, Genesis P-Orridge, formerly Neil Megson, disports his now transgendered body in New York, having been exiled after a born-again Christian campaign against him on (ultimately groundless) suspicion of carrying out illegal occult sex rituals. I am sure my old headmaster Mr Philip Griffiths must feel a twinge of something, hopefully pride.

Nicholas Bullen, The Napalm Deaths' singer and the only member to make it to the band's first album proper, 1987's *Scum* – and the only one still active in music – was not at Solihull School. One of The Napalm Deaths, Darryl Fedeski, had appeared alongside me as a fisherman in a school production of Agatha Christie's *Ten Little Niggers*, which is now rarely produced under its original title due to that political correctness gone mad which they have these days. The other two Solihull School Napalm Deaths, Graham Robertson and Miles Ratledge, were regulars on the Mountain Club walks. The Mountain Club was run by enthusiastic teachers who were also experienced hill walkers, and every other weekend they would transport us west past Telford in a blue minibus to unimagined lunar landscapes, then still strewn with crashed WWII bombers, in far-flung bits of Wales. I ended up president of the club and am eternally grateful to it for the love of the outdoors it instilled in me, for the sense of the sublime, and for it providing the only source of exercise I have as an adult male. Also, the kids in the year above played much better music on the Mountain Club minibus than my friends did, being just old enough to have caught the tailwind of first-wave punk, instead of the New Wave of British Heavy Metal shit my year liked.

I only saw The Napalm Deaths once, at Dorridge village hall in 1982, and wasn't a massive fan, but it was inspiring that people you were on nodding terms with, who were still only fourteen, fifteen,

Richard Hammond was, was five years below me. Despite that, I did know him for a term. Um, and I was very good friends with him for a term. What happened was, one morning I went into this old, um, old toilet, like a pre-war toilet block. No one really used it apart from for smoking and stuff. And there was this young lad in there about eleven years old, and there were three fifteen-year-olds all gathered round him and sort of knuckling him on the head and kicking him and stuff. And I went over, and 'cause I was in the year above they dispersed.* And I said to this little boy,

---

were getting tracks on compilation albums, like Crass's *Bullshit Detector* series, and playing real gigs. Before inventing ultra-fast hardcore, The Napalm Deaths were actually a shouty political band in the vein of Crass or Conflict. Miles the drummer gave me a demo tape called *Punk Is a Rotting Corpse*, which I have now lost. I've been all over the music blogs on the net trying to mainline a hit of anarcho-crusty nostalgia, but there's only a knock-off version masquerading as the real deal. The one with the track 'Traditional Society' on it is what I'm looking for. If anyone's got it, cough up.

A nice boy called Tim Collingwood's brother's Stiff Little Fingers covers band, Nobody's Heroes, headlined over The Napalm Deaths at the Dorridge village hall gig. During their set Pete Davis, who is now a dentist in Christchurch, New Zealand, and I were repeatedly bashed over the head by Dorridge mods, who chased us out of the venue in purple trousers and bowling shoes, which they had stolen from the bowling alley in Hall Green after Paul Weller wore them on *Top of the Pops*. We ran into someone's drive and rang an old man's doorbell, asking if we could use his phone to ring our mums. It was THE PUNK WARS. Kids today don't know they're born.

* I know exactly which toilet this was: left of the fire-escape steps that led up to the art room, where our art teacher once kept my girlfriend behind after lessons to tell her she 'was not like the other sixth-form girls', and opposite the prefab block where we did languages. Intervening in a bullying incident such as the one described

'What's your name?' And he said, 'Richard Hammond.' And I said to him, 'Are you all right?' And he said, 'Not really,' and he looked like he'd been knocked about a bit. And I said to him, 'Does this happen to you a lot?' And he said, 'Pretty much every day.' Er . . . So I said to him, 'Look, I'm the library monitor, right, and you can come and um . . .'

[*The audience laugh at the mention of Stew being a library monitor. Stew walks, disgruntled, to the wings and takes a swig from a bottle of water.*]

Hey, er . . . Now, I did this show, er, thirty times in Edinburgh in the summer, and in Edinburgh the library is not the funny part of this story. OK? I'm not, I'm not having a go, I'm just saying that they don't . . . Way over there, they don't, er, regard the printed word with such . . . I think that's . . . I don't mind. I don't mind. [*walks to wings to return water bottle*] I don't mind what you laugh at, right, I'm happy for anything. But the . . . the thing is, this story's about five minutes long and it takes place in a library, and there's . . . look, there's people walking out there. There's people going home. Everyone's got a cut-off point with taste issues, you know. The Glasgow . . . 'I didn't expect . . .' The Glasgow crowd, 'I didn't expect to come out and hear about the books and words. This is disgusting.' You know . . . It doesn't matter, right, I'm fine, but it's just . . . don't get bogged down laughing at the library in this bit, 'cause the other . . . it's not what it's about. OK, so . . . It doesn't matter.*

---

is exactly the sort of thing I, as a self-righteous fifteen- or sixteen-year-old, would have done.

* I found if I played this with absolute conviction I could micro-manage the audience response to the point where I could stop and drink water, and provoke laughs while I did so, at exactly the same moment every night and have fun making the crowd feel like

So I was the library monitor and, er . . . [*a laugh comes from the area of the room that had previously seemed sympathetic*] Was that over here? This is the part I didn't expect it in. *Et tu!* Yes, that was a reference to Shakespeare, I don't know if you . . . You ever see that? It's about betrayal.

So . . . So I, er . . . Anyway, I said to Richard Hammond he could come in the library any time and they wouldn't come and find him there. He came the next day and he was really nice. He helped me file loads of books away and then he just got on with some little drawings, little funny animals and stuff. And um . . . He did. That's what he was really good at, little . . .*

And then he came back the next day, he came back pretty much every day for the whole of the rest of the term, apart from when he had, er, sport, or army cadets he was in. Um. And he was really nice. And, you know . . . the first couple of weeks he did what any eleven-year-old boy left alone in a library would do. He used to get down all the books about the human body and art and look for nude women in them, you know. And in the end I said to him, 'Look, Richard, you're here every day, you may as well try and read something good.' And I tried to get him to read some of the sort of books I was reading at the time, you

———

philistines. Again, I wasn't the library monitor, but I could picture the library exactly in my mind. For readers of the future, libraries were rooms full of books, many of which were available for the public to use for free.

* I skimmed Hammond's book. He was good at drawing cartoons as a boy, so I brought that in. I never had a brother. I imagined what it might have been like to have a younger friend who might have been a brother, and I imagined that Hammond was that boy. I made myself well up inside, nightly, with the sadness of it, crying for the loss of the brother I never had.

know, like Camus and Sartre and Kafka and things like that.* Ah ha ha ha. And he . . . And he read some of them, and we'd talk about them, and his family, and growing up, and school and stuff. And um, now . . . I, I was from a single-parent family, I didn't have brothers or sisters, and at the risk of sounding mawkish, I think that the, the, the two months that I, um, talked to Richard Hammond every day, erm, were the closest I came to like a sibling relationship, really, in my teens, and I was very grateful to him for the trust, you know. Er . . . Now, the last time I saw him in the library was about a week before the end of term. I was by these glass double doors that went out into the corridor; he was, um, filing some of the books away, and he suddenly went, 'Oh, oh!' And he pointed out in the corridor. And these three kids that had been beating him up were coming. Um . . . Now, I didn't have a key to the door, so I said to Richard Hammond, 'Quick, chuck us the two biggest books on that trolley.' And he did. The first one was a dictionary, the second one was a Penguin paperback edition of *Ulysses* by James Joyce. And I slid those in the handles, and I made like a bolt, and these kids couldn't get in, and they went away. And I think it's ironic, given that Richard Hammond's now a kind of publicly funded cheerleader for mass ignorance, that he was saved by a James Joyce novel.

Now, that was the last time I saw him in the library. He

* The audience would laugh here, at me, because they know enough about people and the world to realise that I was, clearly, exactly that Camus-reading adolescent, plump with the self-importance of it, and that I am still that boy now, and that is why I am onstage in Glasgow, in black jeans and Dr Marten shoes, the John Peel-show teenager, forty-something and fat and still not yet fully grown, a joke figure, a man in denial despite grey hair and children and failing hearing.

didn't come back. I don't know why. But the last time I saw him to speak to was about a week later. I went back to that same toilet, he was there, as were those three kids, but this time they weren't beating him up, they were all sharing cigarettes and they were looking at a, a *Rustler*, which was like a, a porn mag for men with a little, little record on it.* And I said to him, 'Hello, Richard,' and he blanked me. Um, and I went for a wee, and while I was doing the wee, er, one of them said to him, 'Who's that, Richard?' And he said . . . [*removes piece of paper from jacket pocket*†] 'I don't know. It's some queer. Some queer bender from the sixth form who's always trying to feel me up.' [*puts piece of paper back in pocket*]

Now . . . that story about Richard Hammond is not true. But I feel that what it tells us about Richard Hammond is true.‡

That's the main thing, isn't it? Just a bit of fun, you know. [*two audience members leave*] Both going out there.

---

* A ginger-haired boy called Howard could always be relied upon to drip-feed semi-hardcore like *Rustler* into the school's black economy. The *Rustler* flexi disc that did the rounds was called *Pandora's Box*, upon which a woman with a West Country accent told a rude story. My friend Stuart knew the record off by heart and would recite it from the top bunk in the Mountain Club's Snowdonia cottage: 'My name's Pandora and this is my box. Call it a cunt. Call it a fanny. Call it what you will. I calls it my box.' The crate-digger Jonny Trunk has compiled a selection of these pornographic flexi discs on the album *Flexi-Sex*. What would today's young people, with their broadband access to a world of filth, make of such quaint cultural ephemera?

† Another good opportunity to utilise a piece of paper, to give Hammond's supposed words the weight of absolute authority.

‡ This revelation usually provoked an uproarious round of applause, as people enjoyed the audacity of being tricked.

Everyone has a cut-off point. 'I didn't pay to hear a twenty-minute fictional story about Richard Hammond . . . set in a library.'

He is a disappointing figure, though, isn't he? I mean . . . He is. I mean . . . The problem is, it disappoints me. Now, now Frankie Boyle and all the young angry comics, they say that me and the older turns, we should be more angry, you know, like them, about . . . the Queen's vagina he was angry about. He was furious. But . . . my main response to the world is not one of anger, as I get older, I find it's one of disappointment in people like Richard Hammond, or in culture or in government or . . . A, a general disappointment as all the things that I valued as a child have been taken away from me and changed and I can't get them back. And the last thing I want to do tonight is I'm going to tell you a story that hopefully will explain this disappointment, and it normally takes about twenty minutes, so . . . Right. OK. It'll be longer tonight, though.*

Now, disappointment. When I was about sixteen I had a stomach disorder called ulcerative colitis. In my thirties it became something called diverticulitis. The next stage is Crohn's disease, but they've told me that I won't get that, er, which is good. But, um, I was hospitalised with it about six years ago. I went into the Whittington hospital in North London, and they did tests for a few weeks to see if I would have to have a catheter fitted for life and be fed by injection. And at the end of all this I went to see the specialist in

* The show is really settled now. The expectation of jokes is long forgotten, it's clear there will be no crowd-pleasing sick humour or life-affirming everyday observations, and the pace is glacial. In establishing the following story, I once again use a real-life experience, drawn from my ongoing gut traumas, to wrong-foot the crowd with something that feels unimpeachably real.

his room, and he did this thing where they get you, they get the results up on a screen, and then he just looked at them for ages without saying anything. You've probably had this happen. So after a while I said to him, 'Look, you don't have to beat around the bush,' I said to him. 'My mother had Crohn's disease, I've talked to her about coping strategies. So, you know, don't prevaricate. Just give me the results, just give it to me straight, like a pear cider that's made from 100 per cent pears.'*

And he said, 'I'm sorry, what did you just say there?' And I said, 'Look, I'm not trying to tell you how to do your job, but I was on that ward. You know, I talked to all these other guys there about what they'd had, and so don't, you don't need to cushion the blow.' I said to him, 'Just give me the results, just give it to me straight, like a pear cider that's made from 100 per cent pears.'

And he said, 'I am sorry, I've not heard that phrase before.' Er, which struck me as odd, 'cause in my family we use it all the time, we always have done. Er, particularly in my grandparents' generation, you know, four or five times a day: 'Give it to me straight, like a pear cider that's made from 100 per cent pears.' But it was only when that doctor pointed it out, I thought, 'Yes, it is odd. You don't hear . . .' I didn't hear other people saying it, you know. But when I was a kid it was absolutely ubiquitous, it was part of everyday . . .†

* You may already have forgotten it, but in the summer of 2009 the Magners cider advert, in which the Welsh comedian Mark Watson says, 'Give it to me straight, like a pear cider that's made from 100 per cent pears,' was everywhere.

† As I said in the Introduction, for my generation of music fans, doubtless humourless absolutists to a man, adverts were a no-no. There is an eighties LA band I loved, The Long Ryders, who were supposed to be the next REM but then dissolved and disappeared,

though the singer Sid Griffin still makes great bluegrass albums. Years later, having trawled the net, their loss of currency Stateside suddenly makes sense. Apparently, they did a Miller beer advert and, under the tyrannical attitudes of the time, it utterly derailed them. Quotes on the website furious.com, in a piece called 'Perfect Sound Forever', explain:

People felt, when all is said and done, that, how can this band, the Long Ryders, be these hip, cutting edge guys, rebellious, and have songs that are anti-war and questioning this and that and sign up to a big American corporation? And that's a really good question to ask. And the answer is: we needed the money. But our original audience left. They said, 'Hey, you know, the Long Ryders aren't hip anymore. They work for the big American corporation. *Sid Griffin, The Long Ryders*

Here's the band that has sort of this, you know, some political leanings, and all that. And then you're accepting some money from corporate America. So, it was kind of a difficult thing to deal with. We really got hit hard for that. *Stephen McCarthy, The Long Ryders*

Some of our peers and some of our 'underground' fans thought we had betrayed them. People – when you're a band like the Long Ryders that really get out there night after night and slug it out in the trenches – people feel like they own you, like they have a piece of you. They're invested in you. And we had really hardcore fans that were really – they were alternative. It was underground, alternative, whatever you want to call it. It was a little bit more real back then. And people took it very personally. They felt that we had sold out. We didn't feel the same way, you know, in retrospect, maybe. Now, everybody sponsors everything. You know Van presents the Warped Tour. Punk rock bands have sponsorships. It's not what it used to be. *Greg Sowders, The Long Ryders*

I would rather a band do a commercial, so they could pay their rent, and then have the freedom to make the music they want to make. *Steve Wynn, Dream Syndicate*

It ruined their career. Now, suddenly *Spin* magazine writes this

And so many of my most profound childhood memories are attached to that phrase, you know, it's . . . I remember when I was about, er, eight, nine years old, I'd had a little, a Jack Russell as a puppy, and I called it Scarry after the, the kids' writer, Richard Scarry. And then he got this

---

big article – 'The Sell-out of Underground Rock' or something like that, I can't remember. And it mentions this thing. And it completely – what it does, it says that this band sold out, they sold their souls to Miller beer. The guy who wrote the article, I guarantee you that he had never been on tour with a band. He doesn't understand the economics of being in a rock 'n' roll band. He doesn't understand that these bands, they sometimes sleep on people's floors because they don't make enough money. Some people get it in their head that [the underground] is such a fabulous thing, it's on this pedestal. And you can't touch it. And it can't be sold. Well, you have to buy the record, right? You have to go pay a ticket to go see these people perform. It's all commerce. They don't want to look at it as that. But it is commerce. And it has to be, in order to survive. *Phast Phreddie Patterson, music writer*

None of these entirely reasonable views changes the fact that if I'd heard a Long Ryders song in an advert as a puritanical teenager, there's no way I'd still be playing their records today. I would have binned them before they had time to mean anything. (That said, when The Fall's 'Touch Sensitive' turned up in a car advert a few years back, I was older and wise, and I just hoped that whichever members of the transient band wrote the tune got paid.)

To explore this idea in a contemporary way, the notion that a supposedly 'alternative' comedian might have a responsibility to protect the emotional investment of the audience that has trusted him, I fabricated the idea that Watson's cider line, 'Give it to me straight, like a pear cider that's made from 100 per cent pears,' was actually something that, like Steve Earle's 'Galway Girl' or an eighties Long Ryders single, had had a huge emotional importance to me, now betrayed by its placement in an advert.

sort of gastro thing and my dad took him to the vet's, and when he came back from the vet's, um, the dog wasn't with him any more. And I said to my dad, 'Where's Scarry?' And he said, er, 'Well, I'll give it to you straight, like a pear cider that's made from 100 per cent pears: I've had him given a lethal injection.'*

So that's just one example. But there's absolutely . . . There's loads, 'cause it was all the time . . . I mean, I remember when I was about six . . . five, six years old, when I first found out that I was adopted, I remember my mum brought a book back from social services called *Mr Fairweather and His Family*, and the idea was that it explained adoption to young adoptees. And I remember being about ten pages in and then saying to my mum, 'Why have you given me this?' you know. And she said to me, 'Well, I'll give it to you straight, like a pear cider that's made from 100 per cent pears. We're not your real family. But, you know, you're loved.'

And that, that's just two examples. But, in a way, they're not the best examples, 'cause they give the impression that the phrase was only ever used for very sort of traumatic things, and it wasn't. It was . . . It was part of the fun, the

* So I could play this piece with conviction, I would attach the supposed use of the pear-cider phrase to various genuine, and usually upsetting, memories from my childhood. These would invariably be changed each night, depending on which family members might be in the audience, as I had no wish to offend anyone or to make people who didn't understand the process at work, or the point of the piece, think I was cheapening their experience. The first story had initially been about my parents' divorce, but the one thing my mother said about the show, when she saw me for the first time in over a decade in early 2009, was that she wished I hadn't mentioned it. So the dead dog went in instead.

banter of every day, as well, you know. Like your gran would be reading the paper, and you'd say to her, 'What's on telly tonight, Gran?' you know. And she'd go, 'Well, I'll give it to you straight, like a pear cider that's made from 100 per cent pears, it's *Inspector Morse*.'*

It wasn't always that, you know. Er, so that's . . . I hope you . . . Yeah, you see what I mean? It was always there. But I do appreciate it was peculiar to my family, and I was trying to think why that was. Now, I'm not a social historian, but my grandparents were shop-floor at the Cadbury's factory in Birmingham, but before that, before the Industrial Revolution, when people came to the cities, going back thousands of years, um, hundreds of generations, my family had been agricultural workers in Herefordshire, Worcestershire. There's apples there, there's pears, there's cider manufacture. Maybe, um, 'Give it to me straight, like a pear cider that's made from 100 per cent pears,' was something they all said in the fields, you know, for fun. Um. But my family took it with them when they went to the city for work. And somehow it survived. Maybe because my gran had nine sisters and they would have all said it, you know.† I don't know, but what

* I located this imagined incident precisely in my memory. I am sitting on the sofa at my gran's. The fifties print of the German forest is behind me. The paper is the *Birmingham Evening Mail*.

† Way back, my mother's family had been agricultural labourers in the shires. They went east for work, I assume, fanning out in a diaspora along the western fringes of Birmingham. To this day, when I take a train along that edge of the city, the dull place names ring with a magical resonance as I remember my grandparents talking about lost relatives and about their own youthful experiences – Longbridge, Northfield, Kings Norton, Selly Oak. My grandfather and my grandmother were originally shop-floor at Cadbury's, and my grandfather said the factory bell would wake

it means to me is when I hear that phrase, it moves me, not just because of the memories of childhood but also because it's about a bigger thing. It's about the history of ordinary British working people on the move. Yeah? Bear with me. Culturally, yeah, going from the country to the city and experiencing incredible change, social change, but holding onto a little something, a little phrase, a way of thinking that defines them as them. It's about what it means to be a human, I think. And . . . and . . . and let's not forget, those generations before us experienced incredible change. Look at the changes outside here in this last hundred years, you know. In this, just outside this theatre. Incredible.*

And my grandad, you know, he grew up in, in . . . in the fields, you know, and then he learned to swim in the River Severn. He did, in Worcester – . . . He learned to swim in the fields in Worcestershire. But then by 1940 he's an engineer for Lancaster bombers. It's incredible. And actually one of his, his crew was the first crew, one of the first crews to fly over Dresden after the Dresden firebombing, and I

---

him in his bed and he could be up and through the gates minutes later before they shut them. My gran did have nine sisters. My grandfather, according to my uncle, had a brother who went missing, working as a navvy in tents by roadsides the length and breadth of the land, in search of tarmac and adventure. I tried to channel the misty memories I had of these people, these stories, to give this piece a genuine flavour.

Although I've been criticised for being an impersonal act about whom audiences learn very little in real terms, much of my material is personal – deeply personal – but I use the flavour of real experiences to inform the tone and pitch of fabricated ones.

* Here, I intend this idea to sound ridiculously romantic and overstated, and I am daring the audience to laugh in my impassioned face, but I also sort of mean it too.

think that he was traumatised by that. But he didn't talk about it. That generation of men didn't talk about their experiences, you know.*

He talked about it once. And I remember . . . I said to him, 'Grandad, what was it like flying over Dresden after the Dresden firebombing?' And he said, 'Well, I'll give it to you straight, like a pear cider that's made from 100 per cent pears. There was nothing moving down there. Just a dog. And I think that on that, on that occasion what we did to the Germans was wrong.' And I remember my gran interrupted him and she said, 'It's nothing compared to what they did to Coventry.' And he said, 'You don't know what you're talking about, shut up.'†

So I hope you can see from all the little stories that I've told . . . the phrase was always there. It's part of the tapestry of the memory of my family childhood. But that's not why it absolutely means so much to me. It's this other thing that I

---

* I loved listening to my grandad's stories about being a ground-crew engineer in the RAF. They mainly concerned the terrible winds that blew around the bases on the east coast, or contriving ways to pick up damaged planes from American bases in the early morning, so he could snag a superior American breakfast, with eggs and great slabs of bacon. I always meant to record all these stories, documenting a different side of the war. But one never does. And the memories gradually fade. The Dresden story stuck out because it made him angry and upset, despite a lifetime loathing of Germans.
† The detail of the dog is precisely as he told it, and his response to my gran's interruption was as recorded, and was uncharacteristically abrupt. She talked about peeping up from the brick air-raid shelter in the back garden of Arnold Road, watching Coventry, the wattle and daub walls of medieval Coventry, liquidise in the heat. He would have none of it. I told a true story, which meant a lot to me, word for word, and unfailingly it got huge laughs every night. Once more, context is not a myth.

think's applicable to all of us, about people holding onto an idea in the face of change. A figure of speech, a way of looking at the world. And I think it's about what it means to . . . to be, to think, to, to feel. And because of that, that phrase, it means more to me than a poem or a prayer, and if you were to say to me, 'Is there a phrase that defines your life?' I would say, 'Yes, there is. And it is, "Give it to me straight, like a pear cider that's made from 100 per cent pears."' It's . . . about memory, but it's this bigger thing about what it means to be, and it . . . it, it's what I reach to and it defines me.

So . . . You can probably imagine my disappointment . . . when I was, er, watching the television . . . in about May, and an advert come on for this pear . . . pear cider. And a . . . little Welsh lad in it, and he says to the barman, 'Give it to me straight, like a pear cider that's made from 100 per cent p– . . .'

[*Stew is so choked with emotion he cannot finish the sentence. He drops the mic and stands silently at the lip of the stage.*]

[*shouts*] And I'm supposed to believe that that's a coincidence, am I? They heard that. They heard that and they went, 'Oh, let's take that, irrespective of its original context or any meaning or love behind it, we'll take that and we'll use it to sell cider.' 'Give it to me straight, like a pear cider that's made from 100 per cent pears.' You expect me to believe that an advertising creative on hundreds of millions of pounds a year would seriously submit a phrase as cumbersome and unwieldy as that, that is stolen [*jumps off the stage and into the aisle, still shouting*] out of the hearts and minds of ordinary working people with no comeback?*

* Each night, I tried to make this the mother of all auditorium incursions, scoping out the theatre in advance to see if there were short cuts via the stucco plasterwork, straight up the walls into the

There's no comeback for them! Thanks for that, Grandad, thanks for fighting in the war! Thanks! Dig him up, dig his corpse up, rip his heart out, wring it out into a bucket and use it to sell cider! That meant something to someone. That meant something.

[*At this point, Stew starts roaming around the auditorium.*]

What people in advertising have got to understand is the world's not up for grabs, it's not a massive picnic table of all different thoughts and opinions [*leaves the auditorium and starts running up the back stairs of the theatre*] and songs and stories and poems and words people have said and images and memories of things that mattered, of shared little thoughts and traditions and things. It's not all just to be taken and changed and used . . . [*emerges onto the balcony*] Not everything. It's not all . . . Don't light this up! This isn't an entertainment. This isn't to be seen.*

You can't just take things and change them. [*starts edging along the front row*] That's gone, that phrase that mattered to us. That's gone, you can't get it . . . I wanted to teach my son that phrase. And there's no point now. People'll go, 'What's that you're saying?'

And he'd go, 'My grandad said it in the fields, they said it in the war.'

They'll go, 'Shut up, it's in an advert.'

---

boxes and the circle. The bigger the room, the funnier it seemed to be a tiny man, shouting into space.

* The level of emotional intensity here, the sense of wrong, of being personally hurt by a cruel world, is very much indebted to watching Johnny Vegas. Also, like Johnny, I would have a sense of where I was trying to get to every night, in terms of the story and in terms of the geography of the room, but I would chop and change and improvise depending on the hopefully unpredictable events and responses in the room.

That's gone, you can't get it back. You can't.

I'm not mad, by the way, I'm not one of these people who thinks everything's copied off them. I'm not the sort of person that goes, 'Oh, in 1976 I did a drawing of a robot and then *Star Wars* came out.' I could be.

[*to audience member with camera*] There's no need to film this, mate. It's being filmed to be commercially available. There's, there's eight cameras here. What you're doing is shit.

I could be . . . I could feel like that, right. 'Cause when I was about eleven, twelve, right, I used to like reggae music, the reggae. Now back then, 1979, '80, if you liked an artist's work . . . [*shouting at audience member and taking his camera*] You had to buy it in a shop . . . for money. Remember? Remember that? When you used to buy things for money rather than just stealing it off people with all your cameras and downloading stuff. You remember? [*tosses the camera back*] And no, I'm not going to be doing another live DVD after this one. 'Cause it's not cost-effective, is it? 'Cause I can go on the internet and in an afternoon I can find more . . . in an afternoon I can find more where you've all stolen it free off torrent sites than I've sold in the whole time . . . I'll be selling some old ones out of a bucket on the way out. If you like the look of them, just get a handful, walk off with them, that's the same. Colin Dench from . . . he's in, from the video company, he was going, 'I can't understand why yours don't sell better.' I know why it is! Look at you. Look at the people that like me, all with pink hair and stuff, look at you. The fucking liberal intelligentsia of Glasgow down here. All reading the *Guardian*. If a fight breaks out tonight, there's going to be no one to mediate in Glasgow.* Look at you all. All

* This description of my audience comes from Tony Law, who used to use it onstage when supporting me.

the clever people, aren't you, in your chequered shirts, with your pink hair. With your umbrellas. Who has an umbrella, mate? No one. Fucking . . . Sherlock Holmes has come. All the clever people, aren't you? That's who likes me. All the clever people downloading stuff off the internet, stealing it. That's not a problem Michael McIntyre has with his audience. 1.3 million of them queuing up at Christmas to buy his DVD. Like captured partisans digging their own mass grave.

[*Stew edges along to far end of balcony.*]

So, I was in Summit Records, the reggae shop in Birmingham, 1979, 1980. Saturday morning in the Bullring, all Rastas work there. I was queuing up to buy *Handsworth Revolution* by Steel Pulse . . .* Don't wander around at this point, madam! There's no need, is there? To wander around at this point! 'Cause if you've ever seen anything ever, and have any sense of the internal logic of any structured piece of art, this is obviously nearly the fucking end!† [*to cameraman*] Get her, wandering about! Have you got her? Get her, wandering about! I don't top this bit! 'Oh, he came out, he ran around, he falsified a satirical nervous breakdown . . . then he shot his own face off with a harpoon.' This is it! I

* This again is a true memory. These days everything is just a mouse click away, but being a music fan before the internet required a degree of bravery. You had to cross cultural boundaries in pursuit of what you wanted. When you could listen, under your sheets at night, on the police radio frequency to riots bubbling up in the black parts of town, Steel Pulse's *Handsworth Revolution* album seemed incendiary. Today it seems strangely placatory, thoughtful and peaceful, especially when compared to the furious, politicised hip hop that followed in the eighties.

† This line began as an improvisation, but it soon became clear that at least one person a night would try and nip out during this bit, perhaps imagining I couldn't see them because I wasn't onstage, so I could usually whack it in somewhere.

shout here for a bit, I go down there, obviously I use that guitar, then that's it! [*to cameraman*] We'll need a single of that guitar clean for the edit, to make that work.*

So I was in Summit Records, Saturday morning 1979, Rastas, *Handsworth Revolution*, Steel Pulse, and my friend in the queue, James, said to me, 'How's your mum?' And I said, 'Not great, actually, 'cause there's a rat in the kitchen and she doesn't know . . .' Yes! Exactly! And then . . . about eight years later, UB40 . . . Oh, they were from Birmingham, weren't they? And there was two of them Rastas in that. They would've known the ones in the shop, they'd've been their friends. And they had a hit with a 'Rat in the Kitchen'. But that's a coincidence. You'd have to be out of your mind to think that.†

[*Stew exits the auditorium, runs back along down the corridor and climbs down a long ladder, shouting as he goes.*]

But 'Give it to me straight, like a pear cider that's made from 100 per cent pears'? 'Give it to me straight, like a pear cider that's made from 100 per cent pears,' that's copied, that's obviously copied. No one would think of that. 'Give it to me straight, like a pear cider that's made from 100 per cent pears.' [*emerges from the wings back onto the stage*] It's copied. No one would think of that. No one. And what breaks my heart about that . . . [*keeps walking and once again jumps off the stage and into the aisle*] is not only is it

---

* Here I am performing and at the same time trying, inappropriately, to take over the direction of the filming of this show from Tim Kirkby, who I am sure was managing fine.

† It was nice when the audience anticipated what was happening here and realised that I would be blaming UB40 for copying me before I made it explicit. That is my favourite thing in stand-up – not even having to finish a joke. And while we're here, let's take ten seconds to remember how great the first two UB40 albums are.

stolen, it's been stolen all wrong.* 'Cause what we said for thousands of years in the fields, in the sweat of our faces, digging up your fruit . . . was, 'Give it to me straight, like a pear cider that's made from 100 per cent pears.' But the Welsh bloke in the advert, he says, 'Give it to me straight, like a pear cider that's made from 100 per cent *pear*.'

What's . . . What's that? One massive pear? One massive pear making all the cider in the world? A pear you can see from space? It's '*PEARS*', the plural of 'pear' is '*PEARS*'! [*contemptuously*] Pear! No one would say 'pear' when they meant 'p–' . . .

If you were out in the shops and you thought, 'Oh, I wish I had ten pears now,' and you went in the grocer's, but for some reason only understood by you, you'd only say 'pear' when you meant 'pears', the only way you'd get ten pears is if you'd go in and out, over and over again, backwards and forwards, ten times in all different hats and wigs . . . doing all the different accents – English, Welsh, English, Welsh, fluctuating between them, backwards and forwards. You'd say 'pears'. Even the bloke in the advert that says 'pear' for money would say 'pears' in his spare time if he needed to get some pears.

Then a thing comes up at the end: 'Magners Pear Cider, 100 per cent pear' – [*clambers back onstage*] should be '*pears*' – 'nought per cent disappointment.' [*picks up the mic again*] Well, I am disappointed. I'm disappointed 'cause it's stolen out of a dead man's heart . . . because it's stolen wrong – it should be '*pears*' – and because there's no point saying that the cider's nought per cent disappointment if you've already

---

* Jumping back down into the aisle at this point was not something I planned to do, but it got a huge laugh. I suppose it was funny to have struggled once round the whole building and then appear to be so angry that I was about to try and do it all again.

said it's 100 per cent pear. 'Cause you can't have more than 100 per cent of a thing, no matter what they tell you.

And even if you could, which you can't . . . there'd be no point saying the cider was nought per cent disappointment, 'cause you can't make a drink out of a feeling. How does that work, huh? Mr Magners walking around the cider factory . . . 'Hello, lads. [*cracks the mic lead like a whip*] Get in the vat. Trample down all the pear. There must be about 500 pear in there. Trample all the pear down. But don't put any feelings in with the pear. Don't put any disappointment in with the pear.'

'We won't do that, Mr Magners. It's just . . . It's an abstract concept, you can't mix it in. It's just pears.'

'It's pear. Trample down the hundreds of pear. Pour in more pear. There's about four million pear up there. Pour the millions of pear in. Trample down the millions of pear, lads. Trample down all the pear, but don't put any feelings in. Don't put any weird foreign feelings like ennui in it, will you?'

'That's like a French existential despair. We won't put that in. It's just pears.'

'Just pear, lads. Just pear. Trample down all the . . . Do you think you might run out of pear? Don't worry, I've got my secret stash. I've got two pear there and two pear there. That's right, lads. Two pairs of pear. Two pairs of pear. It is confusing, isn't it? But it is right. Just pear, no feelings, no disappointment, no ennui. Don't put any weird . . . Don't put like a lust tinged with regret in there, will you? Like someone in Glasgow might have for a librarian? Just pear.'

'I think you'll find it's "pears", Mr Magners.'

'No. It's "pear". And I think you'll find it's "Mr Magner".'*

* Usually, if I deployed enough physical exertion and shouting throughout the Mr Magners dialogue, I could contrive to make this

Now . . . There was an advert on about eighteen months ago for British Telecom, and the music in it was 'Which Will' by the seventies folk-rock singer Nick Drake. Now, we can't know what Nick Drake was thinking about when he wrote 'Which Will', and we can't ask him 'cause sadly he committed suicide two years after it came out. But whatever the tragic visionary was thinking about when he wrote 'Which Will', it's reasonable to assume that it wasn't cheaper calling options.*

And if you'd asked me at any point in the last ten years, 'What's your favourite song?' I'd always have told you the same thing: it's 'Galway Girl' by Steve Earle. Because about twelve years ago I was at the Glastonbury Festival. About two in the morning my friends took me, sort of against my better judgement really, to the acoustic tent, and this guy came on, Steve Earle, I'd not seen him before, a country singer, and, um, he, er . . . played all his best songs on his own at the guitar, and, um . . . just with a mandolin actually . . . and, and, and the one that really jumped out was 'Galway Girl', I think 'cause, er, of the way it had all these

------

feel like the last line of the show, prompting mass applause, so that the following material had the feel of a reflective coda.

* In 1979, when Island issued *Fruit Tree*, a box-set compilation of Nick Drake albums, Drake's music seemed perfect and unsullied by the world. And for years it remained so, even after his entire catalogue was issued on CD. Drake's baroque folk rock was a secret pleasure, disconnected from an increasingly filthy world. Then, in 1999, 'Pink Moon' was in a Volkswagen advert, and the floodgates opened. Drake's music can give a wistful emotional flavour to almost anything, it seems, from phones to small Volkswagen cars and Vicks cough medicine. Today you have to struggle through a cloud of commercially imposed meanings to try and remember the direct emotional connection these amazing songs once made.

clever little internal rhymes, and it also seemed to be about holding conflicting feelings in balance, and, um . . . and it was just an amazing atmosphere, and so . . . you know, that was my favourite song, after that. And then about three years ago I got married, and my wife's family are from the west coast of Ireland, and what she's like seems to sort of dovetail into that song, you know, so 'Galway Girl' was my favourite song.*

And then . . . about eighteen months ago, Magners cider . . . used 'Galway Girl' in a, a cider advert. So when I hear that song now, I don't think of that amazing night and all my friends and my wife who I love, I just think of loads of actors in curly ginger wigs . . . hopping up and down in a bog, looking for the craic.†

[*Stew puts mic back on stand and fetches guitar.*]

So what I've been doing on this tour, I'm, I'm not a musician, but at the end of every night I've been trying to, er, play, er, 'Galway Girl' as best as I can, er, in the hope that if I perform it enough to people round the place then I will get the memory of doing that. And, um . . . I'll be able to, er, to use that memory to, um, overwrite the advert memory and get my own memory back. Er, don't worry, Glasgow, there's been some unusual responses from you here tonight, but the embarrassment you all seem to feel at

---

* Apparently, I've Irish blood going back four generations. And I'm married into an Irish family. To get the required level of sentiment here, I merely plugged into the cloying mush of weepy nostalgia that now flows naturally through my Irish veins.

† In America, comics get applause for saying they love their wives onstage. Here, it seems like a rather daring thing to do, to risk emotion, genuine feeling. Perhaps the only thing potentially more embarrassing for the punters was the threat that I would now play a straight song, straight.

this point is entirely consistent. A national trend. Basically, no one thinks it's a good idea when a . . . middle-aged comedian reaches for a guitar.

Can we have the singer-songwriter lighting state, please?
[*The lights go to a tight circle.**]

Is that, is that coming out of the . . . Is the guitar in your system? No? It's all right, I pressed a button when I picked that up.

Yeah, it's tense now, isn't it? There's arguably a worse atmosphere here now I've said I'm going to sing a song than it was when I said I wanted Richard Hammond to be decapitated. And it's interesting, that, 'cause there's a lot of largely spurious articles these days about what is the last taboo in stand-up. Is it jokes about race, is it jokes about rape? Er, it isn't. In my experience doing this for five months, the last taboo in stand-up is a man trying to do something sincerely and well. People hate it. Loads of *Top Gear* fans up there going, 'Oh, don't do this. Do some rape stuff, come on. It's Monday. Start the week with a rape joke.'†

Two verses. Anyway, to help me, all the way from Brighton, a special guest. Would you please welcome, on the violin, Nick Pynn. Two verses and then we're out. Thank you very much for your, er, patience here. And for

* If I primed the techs to snap to this state, it would get a huge laugh. If they cross-faded, it didn't. Funny lighting changes. Who'd a thunk it?
† The last taboo in stand-up is a man trying to do something sincerely and well. I suppose, having circumnavigated this idea of what kind of comic I wanted to be, this is what it boiled down to, and it seems broadly applicable. Can any of us stand beside what we do with any degree of pride? Inside contemporary comedy's cushion, stuffed with irony and newly enormous commercial possibilities, what is there? Have we anything, artistically or personally, worth saying?

your patience as well at home, watching the downloaded illegal copy.*

All right. One, two, three, four.†

> And I'll give it you straight
> Like a cider that's made
> From 100 per cent pear . . . s,
> From 100 per cent pears,
> From 100 per cent pears,
> From 100 per cent pears.

> Is there any disappointment in there?
> Is your bread and butter salty with regret?
> Do you ever get the feeling you've been cheated?
> Well, maybe, Johnny, just a bit.‡

> Well, the 'Galway Girl' by Steve Earle

* Nick Pynn is one of my favourite musicians. His album *Afterplanesman* is in my all-time top ten. My wife and I had been quietly obsessed fans of his for some time, seeing his Edinburgh shows every year, and in the end we got to know him through musical comedian Boothby Graffoe. I asked him to duet on 'Galway Girl' at The Stand, and he raised my game considerably, enhancing my rudimentary guitar picking with long, flowing violin lines. Next year he's coming on tour with me, as I commit to trying to do musical comedy for real, the genuine last taboo.
† Here we performed two verses of 'Galway Girl' as well as we possibly could, with, though I say it myself, a sometimes disarming flavour of emotional sincerity. Then, softly and unexpectedly, the chord sequence changed slightly and we bled into the following lament. Delay, delay, delay, delay . . . . and release. Ah!
‡ Here I was thinking of Johnny Rotten's butter advert, and I sang the line 'Do you ever get the feeling you've been cheated' with the same intonation he said it at the end of singing The Stooges' 'No Fun' on recordings of his final gig with The Sex Pistols at Winterland, San Francisco, in 1978.

Was my favourite song,
But they sold it off to a cider ad
And my memories went wrong.
And I'm asking you, son, what's an artist to do
For the kind of money that they offer you?
And I dropped the needle, gave the record a whirl,
But I just can't listen to the 'Galway Girl'.

And Iggy Pop wants to be
He wants to be your dog.*

[*Song ends. Applause.*]

Thank you very much. Nick Pynn all the way from Brighton, a long way north. Thanks for having us here, here at the Citizens Theatre, er, in Glasgow. Thanks a lot, cheers. Good night.

EXIT MUSIC: 'SCUFFLE WITH NATURE' BY THE TAKEOVERS†

---

* The riff at the end apes 'I Wanna Be Your Dog' by The Stooges, whose front man, Iggy Pop, is now advertising car insurance in the company of a puppet of himself, with a company whose policies initially wouldn't stretch to cover musicians.

† When I look back at *If You Prefer a Milder Comedian . . .* today, and particularly this recording of it, I allow myself a certain degree of pride, which I don't for all the material in the three preceding stand-up shows. 2004's *Stand-Up Comedian* reads as an arrogant, sure-of-himself character laying down the law to a crowd he expects to agree with him. Only five years later, the tone of *If You Prefer . . .* is totally different. The comedian is a desperate figure, perpetually on the back foot, all but broken and pleading with a crowd he assumes cannot understand him. In this sense it's closer, in essence, to the definition of clowning as a comic look at the ongoing struggle by mankind to retain its dignity. *If You Prefer a Milder Comedian . . .* appears, with hindsight, to depict a man trying to stay upright, in both senses of the word. My fourth solo show since I came back to stand-up, and I feel like I'm starting to get somewhere. At last.

Afterword

The circumstances under which I toured *If You Prefer a Milder Comedian...*, from 2009 to 2010, were totally different to those surrounding *Stand-Up Comedian*, from 2004 to 2005. I had been on television. This alone put about 40 per cent on the audiences, and it changed the way they perceived me too. But the wider world of comedy, outside my narrow field of vision, was also changing. Beyond the borderlands of late-night BBC2, stand-up on television is suddenly everywhere. It is, finally, the big business the industry had hoped it would be ever since Newman and Baddiel played Wembley Arena in the 'New Rock and Roll' days of the early nineties. Worthy, and experienced, acts like Micky Flanagan or John Bishop became apparent overnight successes, selling out enormous venues after – as far as the casual consumer was concerned – just a few slots on BBC1 or ITV stand-up shows.

But does public mass exposure to stand-up prime people to understand the genre implicitly and to accept greater experimentation with form and content, or does it programme them to accept, in fact, a narrower field of options, the idea of what stand-up can be becoming ossified in the process? Can a television series of stand-up be used to blur the art form's boundaries? And as the stand-up comedian, increasingly, becomes someone who is viewed from a £50-seat in an indoor arena, far away in the distance, and in close-up on a massive screen above the stage, where does that leave me?

Between 2009 and 2011 I recorded two series of *Stewart Lee's Comedy Vehicle* for BBC2. In March 2011, Michael McIntyre announced the biggest stand-up tour in British history, which will see him playing to an anticipated 750,000 fans and is expected to gross £25 million. Booooom! Explosions light up the night sky. That's me there, that sudden shadow. I'm trying to hold my patch of dirt, moving forward in the darkness between the flashes and the flares, crawling between the corpses. In my next book, *TV Comedian*, I'll explain what it's like to be, against all odds, an Alternative Comedian in the age of the supa-stand-up™.

Appendix: Warm Diarrhoea

On Sunday, at 2.26 in the afternoon, a man claiming to be the transport correspondent of the *Daily Telegraph* rang me up asking why I had described Michael McIntyre as 'spoon-feeding his audience warm diarrhoea'. I hung up, assuming it was some weird prank call, like the people who ring me at three in the morning asking when I am going to play Leamington Spa, and wake up the baby. I mean, why would the transport editor of the *Telegraph* be asking me about a line from a routine I did in 2009?

The next day in an article in the *Telegraph*, the transport editor, David Millward, whose last three pieces have been about a flying car, mileage clocks and biofuels, tried his driving-gloved hand at writing about stand-up. He explained how Michael McIntyre was unhappy about comedians making fun of him. I had declined to comment, apparently. It seems the transport editor of the *Daily Telegraph* really does have my mobile number after all. He probably has my PIN number too and will delete important messages in the event of my murder. In the current climate, I now have to change my phone number. Bollocks.

What had happened, it transpires, was this. TV's Michael McIntyre had been on Sunday morning's *Desert Island Discs*, where the presenter Kirsty Young had confronted him, as evidence that he was hated by comedians, with a quote from my act, in which I said he spoon-feeds his audience warm diarrhoea. The line comes 2,673 words into a 27,190-word, 105-minute show, 2009's *If You Prefer a Milder Comedian, Please Ask for One*, which takes McIntyre and the Frankie Boyle/Jeremy Clarkson offence model as polarised extremes of comedy, between which I try to find a third way.

The show opens with me attempting to give audiences what the struggling stand-up Stewart Lee imagines they want, namely a McIntyre-style routine about high-street coffee shops. I cast the audience in the role of baffled onlookers as I try to complete this normal routine, whilst being continually distracted, over a twenty-minute period, by invective and nineties-style pirate whimsy. When the audience fail to respond to me reading out a letter from an angry pirate, I say to them, in desperation:

> You have my sympathy, you know? It's 2010, it's a weird time for stand-up. 'Cause you, you sit at home, don't you, all of you, watching Michael McIntyre on the television, spoon-feeding you his warm diarrhoea. I'm not going to be doing that. I haven't noticed anything about your lives. They're not of interest to me. This is a letter from a pirate. It's not about going to the shops or anything.

I wasn't being interviewed. I was in character. Context, Kirsty Young; you are better than this. As Morrissey said to you on-air, 'Your pretty face is going to hell.'

Later on in the same stand-up show, raging off-mic from a theatre box as part of a fifteen-minute offstage freak-out about how all my DVDs are downloaded illegally by hipsters, I call the millions who queue up to buy McIntyre's 'captured partisans digging their own graves'. The case is overstated, for comic effect. I'm not going to pretend I like McIntyre's work in and of itself, and would hate this piece to be misconstrued as an apology, though I do find much to admire in him as a comedian, and the phenomenon of stadium-sized observational stand-up is, to me, both a fascinating and an amusing oddity. But the way the diarrhoea line was presented to him, shorn of set and setting, does make it read rather differently.

Doubtless someone with a search engine will turn up something horrible, but when I am asked about McIntyre in interviews, as all us comedians are now, I have learned to compliment him on having converted a nation to the idea of stand-up as a viable entertainment option, and usually find a way to leaven any negative comments with positive ones (though these are often edited out), even to the extent of expressing the genuine desire to be allowed to tour all his most famous routines myself, word for word, to see if their very familiarity would lend them to a tonal reinterpretation. (Could the endless noticing of everyday quirks be delivered in such a way as to suggest they were the work of a vengeful and malevolent God, for example?) The onstage Stewart Lee, however, a more bitter man twenty minutes into a failed routine about coffee shops, thinks McIntyre is a purveyor of warm diarrhoea. As well he might.

McIntyre went on, on *Desert Island Discs*, to say how his attendance at the 2009 British Comedy Awards was ruined by comedians making fun of him, and how sad it was because his wife had bought a new dress, and he had won after all, beating me and Frankie Boyle for some spuriously defined gong. I wouldn't know. I wasn't there. I went once in 1992 and I've only been invited once since, when I was working anyway. It's not my bag. I saw it on TV once and there was a big, frightened, unhappy snake writhing around on stage, and loads of drunk TV twats were laughing at it as it flailed miserably towards their coke-flecked tables.

Nevertheless, Monday's *Metro* carried the following headline: 'Michael McIntyre has told of his upset after fellow comedian Stewart Lee insulted him at the British Comedy Awards.' I wasn't at the British Comedy Awards, as I say, but by now the story seems to suggest that, in the moment of McIntyre's triumph, I jumped up, banged the table with my fists, shouted something about diarrhoea and tore his wife's dress. I wasn't there, and yet I'm continually quoted as the focal point of the rudeness that upset him. Is there no one who was actually there who could be named instead? Jonathan Ross mocked him from the Comedy Awards podium, and Lee Mack had recently called McIntyre a 'skipping cunt' onstage in Canterbury. Why don't they mention them instead?

For the record, I have met Michael McIntyre four times. In the spring of 2005 he was hosting a show at *The Tattershall Castle*, where I went to near silence, as I often did at circuit gigs, and he seemed keen and confident. A few weeks later I saw him in the street in Kilkenny, where he said he'd been 'telling everyone how marvellous' I was, like he was the mayor or something. That summer, in Edinburgh, I stood near him and Jimmy Carr in a courtyard, but I don't think we spoke. And at the BAFTAs last year, where you get a better class of TV coke-head, I shook his hand and wished him luck, even though his flamboyant manager had just whispered under his breath to me the half-serious threat, 'Stop making fun of my boy or you might find your career peaks too soon.'

These days I mainly meet other comics at the sixty or

so unpaid charity-benefit shows I do every year, and I never see McIntyre at any of these, so I don't know him. I don't know anyone who knows him. I don't know anything about him. I don't want to. I want to keep him in my imagination as a phenomenon. David Baddiel has warned me, in an unsolicited email, that I am now too well known to do jokes about people because I will meet them and find they are all right really. He has underestimated the full extent of my antisocial nature.

Anyway, today the *Daily Mail* has got hold of the story, so all sense and reason is out of the window now. Their chief rage-monger, Jan Moir, censured in 2009 for her comments about the death of Boyzone's Stephen Gately, wrote a column with the headline, 'Heard the one about the right-on comics who HATE the funniest man in Britain?' There is very little point in trying to reason with the *Daily Mail*, and attempting to do so appears to have driven Robin Ince mad. But once they have written a load of shit about you, it buzzes away in annoyance, ruining your day, and you have to purge it somehow, and so thanks to *Chortle* for the opportunity to squeeze this one out.

Moir's column about 'foul-mouthed left-wing' comics who hate Michael McIntyre is only able to suggest two examples of this 'cabal': me and, bizarrely, Frankie Boyle, the paper's default bête noir. Here we go, point by point, chop chop chop, timber.

Firstly, I am not 'foul-mouthed'. I swear once in the 180 minutes of the first series of *Stewart Lee's Comedy Vehicle*, not at all in the 105 minutes of my last live show *If You Prefer a Milder Comedian . . .*, and only once in the ninety minutes of the previous live show, *41st Best Stand-Up Ever*, when I describe Moir's fellow *Daily Mail* columnist Richard

Littlejohn as a 'cunt' for saying the East Anglian sex-worker murders were of no consequence. Michael McIntyre actually swears more than me.

Apparently I represent 'a slime pit of unpleasantness', and once again the *Mail* decontextualises one line from my forty-five-minute 2009 routine about Richard Hammond to prove this. The same routine also references the anti-PC brigade's attempts to 'upset the grieving relatives of Stephen Gately', an explicit nod towards Moir herself, who either chose to ignore this, didn't understand it or hasn't watched the piece. (You decide.)

Ironically, because people like Jan Moir make it impossible now to employ any degree of comic ambiguity for fear of them choosing to misrepresent it, the DVD of the bit actually ends with the line, to camera:

I don't really think Richard Hammond should die. What I was doing there, as everyone here in this room now understands, just in case there's anyone from the *Mail on Sunday* watching this, is I was using an exaggerated form of the rhetoric and the implied values of *Top Gear* to satirise the rhetoric and the implied values of *Top Gear*. And it is a shame to have to break character and explain that. But hopefully it will save you a long, tedious exchange of emails.

Again, Jan Moir either chooses to ignore what is, essentially, a direct address to her, or else she hasn't watched the bit.

The *Mail* and *Mail on Sunday* writers who hadn't seen the Hammond bit continually misrepresented it in search of scandal, as they did with *Jerry Springer: The Opera*, which I contributed to, but when their own critic finally went to see the show he concluded: 'In context, nothing

Lee says [about Richard Hammond] is offensive.' How about some joined-up thinking?

Moir continues:

Lee claims he was making a point about bullying, but the viciousness is breathtaking. Which brings us to Frankie Boyle, the malcontent Scottish comedian who thinks it is funny to make jokes about child rape, Madeleine McCann and, famously, Katie Price's blind, autistic son, Harvey.

No. What I do does not 'bring us to Frankie Boyle', because I don't do anything about child rape, Madeleine McCann or Harvey Price, or anything like any of that; and it doesn't bring us to Frankie Boyle because he has neither been quoted as commenting on Michael McIntyre nor ever been described as left-wing and PC and liberal, which surely makes him utterly irrelevant to both the title and the supposed content of Jan's silly article. At least this time when the *Mail* has misrepresented me my mother isn't here to be embarrassed by her *Daily Mail*-reading friends, pitying her for having a son who would do and say all these things that I didn't really do or say.

There is no story here, no facts, no names, nothing. Perhaps Jan Moir knows this, and this is why she has appended this Boyle irrelevance to the end of it and conjured a cabal of McIntyre-hating foul-mouthed left-wing comedians, without actually being able to name a single example of anyone who fits this bill. And, prior to Frankie Boyle's joke about Jordan's son, the last time the public spontaneously moved against someone on the grounds of taste and decency, it was against Jan Moir herself. To paraphrase her own comments on Boyle, 'You might think there would not be a rock in the country big enough for

[Jan Moir] to crawl under and disappear for ever.' Moir's piece is diarrhoea. And it's not even warm.

The problem with doing jokes about McIntyre is that it's become a cliché. Everyone's doing them, and by the time I got to record my Michael McIntyre song for TV in January I was already aware it was dead in the water, though thankfully it was cut short by people walking out bored. To quote Simon Munnery, a greater comedian than anyone mentioned on this page, and one who has never won a British Comedy Award: 'When the crowd get behind you, you're probably facing the wrong way.'

But it is necessary for people to be reminded that there is more than one way of doing stand-up, as McIntyre's observational schtick becomes a gold standard and young comics think their only chance of success is to get a slot on his roadshow. I've made the point, in a piece for the *Independent*, that McIntyre's ubiquity means 'alternative' comics do, for the first time since the seventies, have a clearly visible mainstream to define themselves in opposition to, and this has benefited me, for example, enormously, I think. But despite the suggestion that he has been victimised by Frankie Boyle's imaginary liberal cabal, McIntyre is a very powerful figure. Indeed, I once, mistakenly in retrospect, pretended to be Michael McIntyre and, for a joke, rang up a famous comedian who had made fun of him. The panicked fifteen-minute apology he gave me before I'd even had a chance to reveal myself spoke volumes about the influence he is perceived as wielding.

The downside of all this nonsense, apart from having to change my phone number and waste a whole morning during Edinburgh preview season writing this righteous blow-off, is that I would still really love to do a tour reinterpreting Michael's routines, but I expect all this makes that dream even less likely to be fulfilled. On the positive side, my wife worked for the *Daily Mail* as a researcher in the early noughties and, as a punishment for this, whenever it runs a stupid made-up story about something I've worked on, I make her have sex with me. So far the *Mail* has made up stuff about *Jerry Springer: The Opera* and the *41st Best Stand-Up* set, and so now we have two beautiful children. A third will soon be on the way. And I will name him Michael. Michael McIntyre Diarrhoea Lee.

First published on
19 July 2011 on the
comedy website *Chortle*

POSTSCRIPT: Two days after this piece was posted on *Chortle*, the *Daily Mail* removed Jan Moir's original article from its website.

Acknowledgements

I'd like to thank, in no particular order, the promoters of the *If You Prefer* . . . tour, David Johnson, John MacKay and Sally Homer; the opening acts, Tony Law, Henning Wehn and Simon Munnery, for their support, company and input; Nick Pynn for violin accompaniment and guitar tuition; our driver Omri Vitis; my agent Debi Allen; Andy Miller, the editor of this tract; Hannah Griffiths, Ian Bahrami and everyone at Faber; Colin Dench, who released the *If You Prefer* . . . DVD through Real Talent, and Tim Kirkby who shot it; The Stand, Edinburgh, and all her staff, for the usual August workshop run; and my wife, Bridget Christie, for her patience.